Teacher: What can you tell me about the great scientists of the eighteenth century?
Pupil: They're all dead.

Bill: This match won't light.
Ben: What's wrong with it?
Bill: I don't know. It worked all right a minute ago.

Undertaker: Can I help you, sir?
Man: Over my dead body!

Also published by Ballantine Books:

STUPID JOKES FOR KIDS

MORE STUPID JOKES FOR KIDS

BALLANTINE BOOKS • NEW YORK

Copyright © 1989 by Cliveden Press

All rights reserved under International and Pan-American Copyright Conventions. Published in the United States by Ballantine Books, a division of Random House, Inc., New York, and simultaneously in Canada by Random House of Canada Limited, Toronto.

This work consists of portions of *The Great Big Fat Giant Joke Book* originally published by Cliveden Press in Great Britain in 1989.

ISBN 0-345-37061-9

This edition published by arrangement with World International Publishing Limited

Manufactured in the United States of America

First Ballantine Books Edition: June 1991
Third Printing: June 1993

A man rushed into a shop. "Quick, give me a mouse trap," he said.

"I'll be with you in just a minute," said the assistant.

"Hurry, please, I've got a bus to catch," said the customer.

"Oh, I'm sorry, sir, we haven't got a trap big enough to catch a bus," said the assistant.

What would you say to a dead robot?
Rust in peace.

How do ghosts travel?
On fright trains.

Why was the baby corn crying?
He wanted pop corn.

1

What kind of bow is hard to tie?
  A rainbow.

What do you call a back-seat driver with a map?
  A nagivator.

What did the sea say to the sand?
  Nothing. It just waved.

What do invisible people drink?
  Evaporated milk.

Dentist: I'll have to charge you fifteen dollars for taking that tooth out.
Patient: But you said it would only be five dollars.
Dentist: I know, but you screamed so hard that you frightened two other patients away.

Why are the letters N and O very important?
  Because we can't get ON without them.

What does the winner of a race lose?
  His breath.

Why are football players always so cool?
  Because they have lots and lots of fans.

What is the quickest way to get to the bus stop?
  By running.

What do you call that judge with blonde hair?
  A fair judge.

What does Kojak sign his name with?
  A baldpoint pen.

Did you hear about the boy who was called
Seven-and-a-half?
  His father pulled his name out of a hat.

What does a liar do when he is dead?
  He lies still.

Optician: Remember, you must wear your
glasses all the time—even when you're working.
Patient: That's going to be difficult—I'm a boxer.

3

Clown: Boss, boss, the tent's on fire!
Circus manager: Never mind, just bring the fire-eater!

Lady in elevator: Bellboy, I don't like the noises this old elevator is making. If the cables broke, would we go up or down?
Bellboy: That, madam, depends on the kind of life you've led. . . .

Good evening. Here is the news. Earlier today a cement mixer collided with a police van taking prisoners to jail. As a result of the accident the prisoners broke free. Police are now looking for six hardened criminals. . . .

Teacher: What are you going to be when you leave school, Paul?
Paul: Happy.

Knock, knock.
Who's there?
Alex.
Alex who?
Alexplain later—just let me in, will you?

Farmer Giles: That was a terrible storm we had last night, wasn't it?
Farmer Miles: It certainly was. Did it damage your barn?
Farmer Giles: I don't know—I haven't found it yet.

Bridesmaid: Do your feet ache?
Bride: No, why should they?
Bridesmaid: Because everyone says you've been running around after Jim for months.

Guest: May I sit on your right hand at dinner?
Hostess: Wouldn't you be more comfortable on a chair like everyone else?

Why do thirsty men always wear watches?
Because of the springs in them.

Bill: I think blondes are better tempered than brunettes, don't you?
Ben: I don't think so at all—my wife's been blonde *and* brunette, and she was bad tempered as both.

Tommy: What is untold wealth?
Bobby: Money the tax man doesn't know about.

What's black, hairy, and miles from shore?
  An oil wig.

Policeman (to two prisoners): Where do you live?
First prisoner: No permanent address.
Second prisoner: In the apartment above him.

What goes quick quick?
  A duck with hiccups.

How do elephants talk to each other?
  On elephones.

How do you count cows?
  You use a cowculator.

Teacher: What are raised in damp climates?
Pupil: Umbrellas.

Bob: Do you know they're not making lamp-posts any longer?
Bill: Why not?
Bob: They're long enough already.

What is green and stands in a corner?
  A naughty frog.

Mick: When can your pocket be empty, and yet have something in it?
Nick: When it has a hole in it.

What do you give a pig with a sore throat?
  Oinkment.

Salesman: Would you like to buy a pocket calculator?
Customer: No thank you—I already know how many pockets I've got.

Customer: Will you join me in a glass of lemonade?
Barmaid: No, thank you—the glass is too narrow to fit both of us in.

Knock, knock.
Who's there?
Mister.
Mister who?
Missed her at the bus stop.

Mother: Jim, how did this window get broken?
Jim: I was cleaning my slingshot, Mom, and it went off in my hand.

Man: Please call your dog off.
Boy: But I always call him Scamp.

What was Batman doing up the tree?
  Looking for Robin's nest.

Which animals in Noah's ark did not come in pairs?
  Worms, they came in plums.

Knock, knock.
Who's there?
Gino.
Gino who?
Gino me?

What person is always in a hurry?
  A Russian.

What did the big chimney say to the little chimney?
  "You are too young to smoke."

Customer: Do you serve crabs here?
Waiter: Sit down sir, we serve anyone.

Knock, knock.
Who's there?
Dino.
Dino who?
Dino the answer?

Knock, knock.
Who's there?
Alaska.
Alaska who?
Alaska my mommy.

Who never gets his hair wet in a shower?
  A bald man.

Mom: Come on, Sue, eat your dinner.
Sue: I'm waiting for the mustard to cool.

*Did you hear about the boy in the third grade
who does bird impressions?*
  He eats worms for breakfast.

What turns without moving?
  Milk, when it turns sour.

*How many feet are there in a field of three
hundred sheep, three dogs, two cows, seven
horses, and a farmer?*
   Two—all the rest have hooves or paws.

A man went into a bakery. "I want to complain,"
he said. "There was a twig in the loaf of bread
you sold me yesterday."
   "There would be, sir," said the assistant. "We
have branches all over town."

Where do wasps come from?
   Stingapore.

What has a tail that never wags?
   A shirt.

Patient: Doctor, I think I'm going insane.
Doctor: I know how you feel—maddening, isn't it?

*What is the distance between a stupid person's
ears?*
   Next to nothing.

What is smaller than an ant's mouth?
   An ant's dinner.

What is the hardest thing about learning to roller-skate?
   The ground.

Visitor: With so many cows, how can you tell which is which?
Dairy farmer: Oh, I've been milking them for years—I can tell one from the udder.

Lady: My husband did as I asked and bought me a fur this year.
Neighbor: That's nice. What kind was it?
Lady: A Christmas tree.

What did one shrub say to the other shrub?
   I'm bushed!

What happens when you throw a green rock into the Red Sea?
   It gets wet.

What does an envelope say when you lick it?
   Nothing. It just shuts up.

11

Knock, Knock.
Who's there?
Avenue.
Avenue who?
Avenue heard the good news?

Why should you leave your watch at home when you take an airplane?
   Because time flies.

Knock, knock.
Who's there?
Bolivia.
Bolivia who?
Bolivia me, I know what I'm talking about.

Where do frogs sit?
   On toadstools.

Knock, knock.
Who's there?
Boo.
Boo who?
Well, you don't have to cry about it.

What is a hedgehog's favorite food?
   Prickled onions.

Why do bears have fur coats?
  They'd look silly in leather jackets.

What do you call a parrot in a raincoat?
  Polly unsaturate.

Why did the two elephants go for a swim?
  Because they wanted a pair of swimming trunks.

A truck carrying hair restorer was stolen from outside a cafe.
  Police are combing the area.

Customer: Waiter, there's a button in my salad.
Waiter: Quite right, sir, it's part of the dressing.

Door-to-door salesman: Just give us a small deposit, Madam, and then you'll pay nothing for the next six months.
Woman: Who told you about us?

Which burn longer—the candles on a boy's birthday cake or the candles on a girl's birthday cake?
  Neither, all candles burn shorter.

13

How do you know when a fish is deaf?
  It wears a herring aid.

What's black and white and red all over?
  A very embarrassed zebra.

Priest (to a tribe of cannibals): On Fridays you must eat fishermen.

Did you hear about the man who got a job sweeping leaves in the park?
  He fell out of the tree and broke his leg.

Did you hear about the old lady who kept her canary in a goldfish bowl?
  A friend asked her why she didn't keep it in a cage.
  "I tried that," she said, "but the water kept coming out."

Jim: Look at that flock of cows.
Tim: Not flock, herd.
Jim: Heard of what?
Tim: Herd of cows.
Jim: Of course I've heard of cows.
Tim: I mean a cow herd.
Jim: A cow heard? So what, I didn't say anything I shouldn't have, did I?

Author: It took me six years to write my book.
Ex-convict: So what? It took me twenty years to complete a sentence.

Customer: Four bars of soap, please.
Shop assistant: Scented?
Customer: No, I'll take them with me.

Teacher: Matthew, can you take five from one?
Matthew: Of course I can.
Teacher: How can you manage that? Explain it to me.
Matthew: It's easy. I do it every night when I take five toes from one sock.

Referee: I'm booking you for a late tackle.
Fullback: That's not fair, I couldn't get here any faster.

What do you call a missing container?
  Jargon.

Why is a dog warmer in summer than in winter?
    In winter he has a coat, in summer he has a coat and pants.

Why do hungry people go to the desert?
    For the sand which is there.

Why did the nosey neighbor look over the wall?
    Because she couldn't see through it.

Jane: What's the difference between an orange, and an elephant and glue.
Jack: You can eat an orange and you cannot eat an elephant, but what about the glue?
Jane: I thought that's where you'd get stuck.

Knock, knock.
Who's there?
Duane.
Duane who?
Duane the bathtub, I'm dwowning.

What happens if you give your cat a lemon?
    You get a sour puss.

Why did the chicken swear?
  Because it only knew fowl language.

Knock, knock.
Who's there?
Sincere.
Sincere who?
Sincere light was on, I thought I'd call.

Why do doctors wear masks during operations?
  So that if one of them makes a mistake the others won't know who to blame.

Customer: What flavor ice cream do you have?
Waitress (whispering): Vanilla, strawberry, chocolate, mint, lemon, orange, tutti frutti, and toffee.
Customer: Do you have laryngitis?
Waitress: No, just vanilla, strawberry, chocolate, mint, lemon, orange, tutti frutti, and toffee....

Why do some people put rollers in their hair at night?
  So they can wake up curly in the morning.

Where do hamsters come from?
  Hamsterdam.

What's big, green, and sits in a corner all day long?
  The Incredible Sulk!

Why is a coward like a leaky tap?
  Because they both run.

What was the first smoke signal ever sent?
  Help, help, my blanket is on fire!

If a man can beat the drums in his ears,
  Or cross the bridge of his nose,
Surely he can tile the roof of his mouth
  Using the nails on his toes?

Mailman: Could this letter be for you? The address is yours, but the name is obliterated.
Resident: It's not mine then—my name is Smith, and I don't know anyone around here called Obliterated.

Wife: I've got a lot of things I want to talk to you about.
Husband: That's good—you usually want to talk to me about a lot of things you haven't got.

Policeman: Didn't you hear me yell "stop?"
Driver: Er, no, I didn't.
Policeman: Didn't you see me signal for you to stop?
Driver: Er, no, I didn't.
Policeman: Didn't you hear me blow my whistle?
Driver: Er, no, I didn't.
Policeman: I might as well go home, I don't seem to be doing much good around here.

What do you call a man with a car on his head?
  Jack.

Why did J.R. go to court?
  To Sue Ellen.

Patient: Doctor, Doctor, will you help me out?
Doctor: Yes, how did you get in?

What kind of ears does an engine have?
  Engineers!

What is black and gushes out of the ground swearing?
  Crude oil.

What do you call a girl standing between two goalposts?
   Annette.

What is never used until it's broken?
   An egg.

Knock, knock.
Who's there?
Cows.
Cows who?
Cows go "moo" not "who."

A cabbage, a tap, and a tomato had a race.
   How did it go?
   The cabbage was ahead, the tap was running,
and the tomato tried to ketchup!

What can you break without even touching it?
   A promise.

Why do bees have sticky hair?
   Because they have honeycombs.

How do you get rid of an old boomerang?
   Throw it up a one-way street.

What do you call a man with a sea gull on his head?
   Cliff.

Workman: Have you seen this morning's paper?
Foreman: Why, what's in it?
Workman: My lunch.

Teacher: You missed school yesterday, didn't you, Tommy?
Tommy: No, not one bit.

If a horse wears shoes, what should a camel wear?
   Sandals.

When did the first two vowels appear?
   Before *U* or *I* were born.

What did the beaver say to the tree?
   It was nice gnawing you.

Why must you be strong to be a policeman?
   You must be able to hold up a line of cars with one hand.

Where did Noah keep his bees?
  In the ark hives.

Girl: Why are you writing with a hot dog?
Boy: Oh no, I must have eaten my pencil for lunch.

How do you start a flea race?
  One, two, flea!

Who's that at the door?
  A man with a drum.
  Tell him to beat it.

What do you get if you cross an owl with a skunk?
  A bird that may smell but doesn't give a hoot.

Why did the one-handed man cross the road?
  To get to the secondhand shop.

If a blue house is made of blue bricks, and a red house is made of red bricks, and a yellow house is made of yellow bricks, what is a greenhouse made of?
  Glass.

What did the tree say to the woodcutter?
  Leaf me alone.

What's the difference between a schoolboy and a fisherman?
  One hates his books, the other baits his hooks.

Teacher: What do you want to be when you graduate?
Pupil: A puppeteer.
Teacher: That should be easy, you'll just have to pull a few strings.

Why did the taxi driver give up his job?
  Because people kept talking behind his back.

Why do you put a sugar lump under your pillow at night before you go to sleep, Sally?
  Because I want to have sweet dreams.

What ring is never worn?
  The ring of a doorbell.

Jim: Dad, can I have five dollars to give to a little old man, please?
Dad: Where is he?
Jim: In the ticket booth at the movie theater.

Teacher: Does anyone in the class have a favorite saying?
Angela: Yes, I do.
Teacher: What is it?
Angela: Let bygones be bygones.
Teacher: That's an interesting choice. Why did you choose it?
Angela: Because if we all took notice of it we wouldn't have to have anymore history lessons.

Passerby: Aren't you lucky, catching so many fish?
Fishing tramp: Lucky? Don't make me laugh! I'm trying to catch a pair of old boots!

Policeman: When I saw you driving by I thought, sixty at least.
Woman: Don't be rude, officer—I'm only forty-five.

Knock, knock.
Who's there?
Ken.
Ken who?
Ken who lend me a dollar till next week?

Man to hotel porter: Run up to my room and see if my coat's still there, will you? It's room 610 on the sixth floor. Hurry, I've got a train to catch, and the elevator is out of order.
Porter (some minutes later): Yes, sir, your coat is still there—it's hanging in the wardrobe.

What happens if you cross a galaxy with a toad?
  You get star warts.

Why did the bald man go for a long walk?
  To get lots of fresh 'air.

What's a frog's favorite food?
  Lollihops.

Why was the fish in a bird cage?
  Because it was a perch.

Which flowers grow on walls?
  Wallflowers.

Knock, knock.
Who's there?
Luke.
Luke who?
Luke through the keyhole and you'll see.

How do you keep cool at a football game?
  Stand next to a fan.

What do you get if you cross a bear and a kangaroo?
  A furry coat with big pockets.

Why did the tomato blush?
  It saw the salad dressing.

What happened to the boy who ran away with the circus?
  The police made him bring it back.

26

How do you keep an idiot in suspense?
  I'll tell you next week.

Gamekeeper: There's no fishing allowed here.
Boy: I'm not fishing, I'm washing my pet worm.

Why don't snakes understand jokes?
  Because you can't pull their legs.

Customer: Waiter, what kind of pie did you bring me?
Waiter: What does it taste like?
Customer: I don't know.
Waiter: Then what difference does it make?

Why is a garden like a story?
  They both have plots.

How can a leopard change its spots?
  By moving to another place.

Knock, knock.
Who's there?
Europe.
Europe who?
Europe to no good.

What is the best year for a kangaroo?
  A leap year.

Why did the man climb up to the chandelier?
  He was a light sleeper.

What is the difference between a bottle of medicine and a rug?
  One is shaken and taken, the other is taken and shaken.

How do you stop a fish from smelling bad?
  Cut its nose off.

What's yellow and goes slam slam slam slam?
  A four-doored banana.

What's black and white and red all over?
  A sunburned penguin.

What is a monster's favorite soup?
   Scream of tomato.

Where did Sir Lancelot study?
   At knight school.

Why did Robin Hood rob the rich?
   Because the poor had nothing worth stealing.

Boss: Why are you so late this morning?
Worker: I fell down the stairs.
Boss: Well, that shouldn't have taken you long to do. . . .

Hey, who do you think you're pushing?
   I don't know—what's your name?

Will February March?
   No, but April May before June.

Why is the sky cleanest in New York?
   Because it has so many skyscrapers.

Hello, is that 2222222? Good—could you phone 911 and ask for a doctor to come at once? I've gotten my finger stuck in the dial. . . .

Why do ghosts have so much fun?
Because they're high spirited.

What's the best way to catch a squirrel?
Climb up a tree and act like a nut.

Why did the teacher wear dark glasses?
Because the class was so bright.

What happens if you dial 116?
A police car arrives upside down.

Did you hear the joke about the wall?
I won't tell you, you'd never get over it.

30

Knock, knock.
Who's there?
Watson.
Watson who?
Watson television tonight?

Knock, knock.
Who's there?
You.
You who?
Did you call me?

*How do you divide four potatoes among five
people?*
Mash them.

*What would you get if you blew your hairdryer
down a rabbit hole?*
Hot cross bunnies.

Visitor: And what will you do, dear, when
you're as big as your mother?
Little girl: Diet.

Which are the last teeth to appear in the mouth?
False teeth.

Knock, knock.
Who's there?
Stan.
Stan who?
Stan back, I'm going to sneeze.

Teacher: I asked for a two-page essay on milk.
You've only handed in two lines.
Pupil: Yes, I wrote about condensed milk.

Mother: Why don't you go and play football
with your little brother?
Boy: He doesn't like it, Mom, and I'd rather have
a real football.

Owner: My dog plays chess with me.
Stranger: It must be a very intelligent animal.
Owner: Not really. Today I've won four games
out of six.

When is a tennis player like a good waiter?
  When he gives a fast serve.

Knock, knock.
Who's there?
Alex.
Alex who?
Alex the questions around here.

Why is a leg of pork like an old radio?
  Because you get crackling from both.

What happens when vampires get together?
  They drive each other batty.

What happens in a vampire horse race?
  They finish neck and neck.

Patient: Doctor, I've got a pain in my left leg.
Doctor: Don't worry about it, it's just old age.
Patient: But doctor, I've had the right leg just as long, and it doesn't hurt at all!

Patient: Doctor, I just can't sleep at all. I have terrible insomnia. What shall I do?
Doctor: Sleep nearer the edge of the bed and you'll probably drop off more easily.

Why is a clock like a condemned man?
  Its hours are numbered.

What bolt will you never find on a door?
  A thunderbolt.

First patient: Is your dentist careful?
Second patient: Oh yes, he filled my teeth with great pains.

Mother: David, have you filled the pepper shaker for me? I asked you to do it hours ago.
David: I know, Mom, but it takes a lot of time to push the pepper through these little holes.

Wife: My husband thinks he's a TV antenna, Doctor.
Doctor: Now don't you worry, Mrs. Jones, I think I'll be able to cure him for you.
Wife: But I don't want him cured, Doctor—I want him adjusted so that I can get Channel 4.

What question can never be answered by the word "yes"?
   Are you asleep?

Comedian: I object most strongly to having to go on stage after that monkey act.
Manager: I don't blame you—the audience will think it's an encore.

What always runs along the street?
   The pavement.

What eats spinach and makes trousers?
    Popeye the tailorman.

Why is mayonnaise never ready?
    Because it's always dressing.

Why did Dracula take some medicine?
    To cure his coffin.

A boy telephoned the doctor's office and urgently asked to speak to the doctor. When he was connected, the boy asked the doctor to come as quickly as he could, as the front door was jammed. The doctor was puzzled. "You need a handyman, not a doctor," he said.

"No we don't," said the boy. "Dad's fingers are in the door!"

What is the definition of a waste of time?
    Telling hair-raising stories to a man who is bald.

Foreman: Come on, get a move on with that bricklaying.
Bricklayer: Rome wasn't built in a day, you know.
Foreman: That's because I wasn't the foreman on the job.

Neighbor: If you don't stop playing that trumpet of yours, I'll go crazy!
Musician: Too late, I stopped an hour ago!

Customer: Waiter, there's a tiny beetle in my soup.
Waiter: I'm sorry about that sir, shall I change it for a bigger one?

What do you call a man with a spade in his hand?
   Doug.
What do you call a man without a spade in his hand?
   Douglas.

Teacher: Give me a sentence with "analyze" in it.
Peter: Anna says she never eats candy, but Anna lies.

Name a car that starts with T.
   None of them do, they all need gas.

Knock, knock.
Who's there?
Arfer.
Arfer who?
Arfer got.

Why did the garden fence?
   Because it saw the window box.

How do you stop moles from digging up the garden?
   You hide their spades.

What do birds eat for breakfast?
   Shredded tweet.

What sort of robbery is the easiest?
   A safe robbery.

Fred: I don't know what to buy my wife for her birthday.
Ed: Why don't you ask her what she wants?
Fred: I don't want to spend that much.

Customer: Lovely weather we're having.
Fortune-teller: Yes, it reminds me of the summer of 2001.

Knock, knock.
Who's there?
Ya.
Ya who?
I didn't know you were a cowboy.

Where do tadpoles change into frogs?
   In the croakroom.

Bill: I always say that people should sleep with a window open.
Will: Oh, you're a doctor, are you?
Bill: No, a burglar.

Knock, knock.
Who's there?
Scot.
Scot who?
Scot nothing to do with you.

What did the earwig say when it fell off the cliff?
   Earwigo again.

Why do witches ride on brooms?
   Because vacuum cleaners are too heavy.

Will the person who took the thruway to New Jersey please bring it back?

Doctor, doctor, I feel like the worst fisherman in the world.
   Don't worry—it's not catching.

What did one dandelion say to the other dandelion?
   Take me to your weeder.

Did you see that boy burying his radio in the park? Why do you think he did it?
   Because his batteries were dead.

Patient: Doctor, doctor, I feel like a wizard.
Doctor: I think you could do with a spell in the hospital.

Patient: Doctor, doctor, I feel like a snail.
Doctor: Don't worry—you just need to be brought out of your shell a little.

Shall I stick these stamps on myself?
   No, Madam, stick them on the envelope.

Teacher: Can anyone tell me what illegal means?
Tony: I can, it means a sick bird.

What kind of pets are always underfoot?
   Carpets.

Mrs. Jones: I've bought a new hat—I always buy one when I'm down in the dumps.
Mrs. Smith: Really! I didn't know they sold hats in the dumps.

Teacher: When is the best time to pick apples?
Pupil: When the farmer's dog is tied up.

Sam: Do beavers bark, Dad?
Dad: No, son, why do you ask?
Sam: Because it says in this book that beavers eat grass and bark.

Mom: What are you doing?
Bob: Washing myself, of course.
Mom: Without soap and water?
Bob: Haven't you heard of dry cleaning?

How did you come to fall in the river?
  I didn't come to fall in the river, I came here to fish!

Teacher: Name?
Tom: Tom.
Teacher: Say Thomas, not Tom. Next boy. Name?
Jack: Jackass.

I thought you said you only had clothes in this suitcase?

That's right—that's my nightcap.

Circus manager: We've got to find someone to replace the sword swallower.
Boss: Why, what's wrong with him?
Circus manager: He says he's fed up to the hilt.

What kind of person would be a good money-lender?

Someone who takes a lot of interest in his work.

How would you describe a press photographer?
A flashy guy.

Patient: Doctor, I was playing my flute and I suddenly swallowed it.
Doctor: Well, look on the bright side. It could have been a grand piano.

Did you hear about the poultry farmer who mixed cocoa with the chicken feed so that they could lay chocolate Easter eggs?

Customer: May I have a table for dinner, tonight?
Waiter: Yes, sir—roast, boiled, or fried?

What do you call a man who works on bridges?
  Archie.

Why are boomerangs popular?
  They're always making a comeback.

Why are fishing stories hard to believe?
  Because there's usually a catch in them.

Why was Count Dracula glad to help young vampires?
  Because he liked to see new blood in the business.

Why should a man's hair turn gray before his mustache?
  Because it is older.

What did the cavemen read?
  "The Prehistoric Times."

Salesman: This hair tonic will grow hair on a golf ball.
Customer: Who wants hair on a golf ball?

An eight-foot-tall patient has been admitted to the local hospital.
He is one of their longest sufferers.

What happened when the housekeeper's husband came in late one night?
She wiped the floor with him.

Knock, knock.
Who's there?
Abyssinia.
Abyssinia who?
Abyssinia behind bars one of these days.

Teacher: Which bird does not build its own nest?
Johnny: A cuckoo.
Teacher: Very good, how did you know that?
Johnny: Everyone knows a cuckoo lives in a clock.

Box office manager: This is the tenth ticket you've bought.
Customer: I know, but there's a girl in there who keeps tearing them up.

What can't you have until it's been taken?
Your photograph.

43

*Why should a golfer keep a spare pair of
trousers?*
   In case he gets a hole in one.

Knock, knock.
Who's there?
Olive.
Olive who?
Olive here so let me in.

*What happened to the man who put his false
teeth in backwards?*
   He ate himself.

Milly: Can I have some of your doughnut?
Billy: Of course—you can have the hole in the
middle.

What can you hold—without touching it?
   Your breath.

*What does it mean when you find a horseshoe,
Farmer Giles?*
   Some poor horse is wandering around in his
socks.

Teacher: Can anyone tell me what an octopus is?
Pupil: An eight-sided cat.

What sort of ship did Dracula captain?
  A blood vessel.

Joiner: You hammer nails like lightning, Jim.
Jim: You mean I'm really fast, boss?
Joiner: No, Jim, I mean that you never strike the same place twice.

You would be a good dancer if it weren't for two things—your feet.

Why did the bald man paint rabbits on his head?
  Because from a distance they looked like hares.

Policeman: Pull over, madam.
Woman driver: No, I'm knitting a pair of socks, officer.

Bill: The collar on this shirt is far too tight for me—it's choking me.
Will: No wonder, you've got your head through a buttonhole!

Teacher: Give a sentence containing an object, Mark.

Mark: You are very beautiful.

Teacher: Well, Mark, that certainly is a sentence, but what is the object?

Mark: A good report card at the end of the semester.

Why wouldn't the pen write?
  Because it was full of pigs.

What's white, fluffy, and beats its chest in a cake shop?
  A meringue-utan.

What can you serve but not eat?
  A tennis ball.

Girl (in line outside concert hall): I wish I'd brought the piano with me.

Boy: What for?

Girl: The tickets are on top of it.

What looks like half a loaf of bread?
  The other half.

Patient: I keep getting pains in my chest.
Doctor: Well, don't breathe so often.

What kind of men can go to a girl's head?
  Hairdressers!

Which was the first fish to go into space?
  A starfish!

Undertaker: Can I help you, sir?
Man: Over my dead body!

Agent: So you're a four-piece band, are you?
Musician: That's right, we only play four pieces!

Connie: It's gotten very quiet in the other room.
Peggy: Yes, I think Bert must have told a joke!

Tom: My sister is a girl with rare talents.
Tim: What can she do?
Tom: Nothing!

When was Louis XVI born?
  On his birthday!

What would you look like if you put your hands in front of your face?
  A clock!

What's green with a trunk and two legs?
  A seasick tourist.

Who tells jokes about knitting?
  A nit wit.

Knock, knock.
Who's there?
Abba.
Abba who?
A banana.

What always follows a dog?
  Its tail, of course.

Where do astronauts leave their spaceships?
  At parking meteors.

Where are the kings and queens of England usually crowned?
  On their heads.

What's the difference between a whale hunter and a happy dog?

One tags his whale, while the other wags his tail.

Knock, knock.
Who's there?
Percy.
Percy who?
Persevere and you might find out.

What bus sailed the seas?

Colum-bus.

Mommy, Mommy, all the boys at school say I look like a werewolf!

Shut up and comb your face.

Ed: I've just bought myself a wig. Do you think I should tell my wife?
Ned: No—keep it under your hat for a while.

What is hairy and coughs a lot?

A coconut with a cold.

What must you always keep—especially when you've given it to someone else?
Your word.

What do you get if you cross a rose with a crocodile?
I don't really know—but I wouldn't want to smell it!

What do you give someone who has everything?
Penicillin.

Did you hear about the two burglars who stole a calendar?
They each got six months.

First mom: My Eddie will have to start thinking about getting a job soon.
Second mom: Has he a particular lean for anything?
First mom: Only on walls and tables.

What is the simplest way to increase your bank balance?
Look at it through a magnifying glass.

First octopus: I don't know what to buy my husband for Christmas.
Second octopus: Do the same as I did for mine and get him four pairs of gloves.

Father: Don't reach across the table. Haven't you got a tongue?
Son: Yes, but my arms are longer.

Did you hear about the man who drove his car off the edge of a cliff to test the air brakes?

Dan: Do you like going to school, Dave?
Dave: I like going to school and I like coming home from school—it's the bit in the middle that I hate.

What did the goat say after it ate a roll of film?
   I liked the book better.

When does a man have four hands?
   When he doubles up his fists.

Why did the fireplace send for the doctor?
   Because the chimney had the flu(e).

Troop leader: One of the things you'll learn about in Scouts is how to make fires out of doors.
Scout: That sounds like fun—where do we get all the doors from?

What is black and white and has sixteen wheels?
  A zebra on roller skates.

Teacher: You're late again. What's your excuse this time?
Smith: I ran so fast I didn't have time to think one up.

Did you hear about the truckload of wigs that was stolen?
  Police are combing the area for clues.

How do you get in touch with a fish?
  Drop him a line.

What do you call a sheep that's just been sheared?
  Bare, bare, back sheep.

Why do men get paid extra for working on top of Big Ben?
   Because they're working overtime.

What is worse than a snake with sore ribs?
   A centipede with athlete's foot.

Why is Sunday the strongest day?
   All the others are week days.

One cannibal to another: Am I late for supper?
   Second cannibal: Yes, everyone's already eaten.

First Man: Every day my dog and I go for a tramp in the woods.
Second Man: Your dog must enjoy that.
First Man: He does, but the tramp's getting fed up with it.

Why can't a bike stand up by itself?
   Because it's two tired.

What's purple and flies?
   Super Grape.

53

Benny: This match won't light.
Johnny: What's wrong with it?
Benny: I don't know, it worked a minute ago.

What do shortsighted ghosts wear?
  Spooktacles.

Knock, knock.
Who's there?
Noise.
Noise who?
Noise to see you.

What happened when the snake got a cold?
  She adder viper nose.

How do you catch a rabbit?
  Stand behind a tree and make a noise like a carrot.

What do you call a cow eating grass?
  A lawn mooer.

Why are they building such a high fence around the graveyard?
    Because everyone's dying to get in.

Why are enemies like loose pages in a book?
    They keep falling out.

It takes about a thousand nuts and bolts to put a car together, but just one nut to scatter it all over the road.

I ate an egg once that wasn't cooked.
    Ugh! What did it taste like?
Great—it was a marshmallow Easter egg!

Joe: I spent ten hours over my math homework last night.
Flo: Ten hours!?
Joe: Yes, I put the book under my mattress!

Gillian: I wonder what that hippopotamus would say if it could talk.
Lillian: It would probably say, pardon, me, but I'm a rhinoceros.

Fred: Did you have a lot of money left at the end of your vacation?
Freda: No, but I had a lot of vacation left at the end of my money.

What makes a hat talk?
   Add a letter *C* and you make it chat.

Hey, what are you doing with your hand in my pocket?
   Sorry, mister, it was just absentmindedness—I once had a pair of trousers just like yours.

What has everyone seen but will never see again?
   Last night.

Grandma: Remember this motto, Julie. Never put off till tomorrow what can be done today.
Julie: Okay, Grandma, that makes sense. We'd better eat the rest of the cake, then.

What goes into water white and comes out black?
   A baker's shoe.

What goes into the water pink and comes out blue?
   A swimmer on a cold day.

I want to send a telegram to Washington.
  You can't.
  Why can't I?
  Because Washington's dead.

Why does a tall man eat less than a small man?
  Because he makes a little go a long way.

What do you call an elephant with no teeth?
  Gumbo.

It was during the Battle of Britain, and the Smith
family, after hearing the air raid warning sirens,
were making their way to the underground
shelter. Suddenly Mrs. Smith stopped. "I'll have to
go back," she said, "I've left my false teeth
behind!"
  Mr. Smith pulled her into the shelter. "Forget
your false teeth, woman," he said. "They're
dropping bombs, not meat pies!"

Have you ever been bitten by an ant?
  No, but my uncle smacked me once.

*Why doesn't Sweden send to other countries for
cattle?*
  Because she keeps a good Stockholm.

Little boy: I want fifty cents' worth of bird seed, please.
Saleslady: How many birds have you got dear?
Little boy: None, but I want to grow some.

Safari guide: Now remember, as soon as you see the leopard, shoot him on the spot.
Gamehunter: Which one?

What is the best shark repellent known to man?
  The Sahara Desert.

What goes clomp, clomp, clomp, clomp, clomp, clomp, clomp, squoosh?
  An octopus with one shoe off.

What's brown, has a hump, and lives at the North Pole?
  Rudolph, the Red-Nosed Camel.

Have you heard about the old missionary?
  He gave the cannibals their first taste of Christianity.

First man: I've changed my mind.
Second man: That's good. Does the new one work any better?

Teacher: Now, if you bought fifty apples for ten cents, what would each one be?
Pupil: Rotten—at that price they'd have to be.

First policeman: I can't understand how those bank robbers got away. Were all the exits guarded?
Second policeman: Yes. They went out by the entrance.

Knock, knock.
Who's there?
Rhoda.
Rhoda who?
"Row, row, Rhoda boat . . ."

Customer: Waiter, I've been waiting half an hour. Will the pancakes be long?
Waiter: No, sir, round!

Customer: Waiter, does the water always come through the roof like this?
Waiter: No, sir. Only when it rains.

Knock, knock.
Who's there?
Police.
Police who?
Police let me in.

Mayor: What do you think of our village band?
Old man: Yes, I think it ought to be.
Mayor: Ought to be what?
Old man: Banned.

First man: Why are you standing in that bowl of water?
Second man: It's the pills I'm on—they're to be taken in water, three times a day.

What lies around all night with its tongue out?
  A shoe.

What smells most in the zoo?
  Your nose.

Why did the teacher carry a ruler with him to bed?
  Because he wanted to know how long he slept.

Sire, I want your daughter for my wife.
  Oh, really? You can just tell your wife she can't have her.

How did the octopus go into battle?
  Well armed.

What does a bird use in an emergency?
  A sparrow-chute.

Bill: I know everything there is to know about soccer.
Jill: Oh, you do, do you? How many holes are there in a goal net, then?

A customer was sitting in a restaurant after eating his meal. When the waiter brought his bill the man read it:

OMELETE	1.25
TEA	.40

  "Take this back," said the customer to the waiter, "and write it again so that it reads omelette with two t's."
  A few minutes later the waiter returned with a new bill, and the customer looked at it. It read:

OMELETE	1.25
2 TEAS	.80

Did you hear about what happened at the flea circus?
  A cat walked in and stole the show.

Why does a hairdresser never shave a man with a glass eye?
Because it's much easier if he uses a razor.

What can't you do with a sack of potatoes in the fridge?
Close the door.

Why is venison always expensive?
Because it's always dear.

What is small, round, white, and giggles a lot?
A tickled onion.

Actress: Do you think my latest movie will change peoples' lives?
Critic: It might—after all, your last movie changed two theaters into bowling alleys almost overnight.

Why did Smith burn his overcoat?
He wanted a blazer instead.

What happened when the couple tried to kiss in dense fog?
   They mist.

Aunt: Well, Joey, how do you like school?
Joey: Closed.

What does the vegetable garden say when you tell it a joke?
   Hoe-hoe-hoe!

"Now, children," the teacher said, "there's a wonderful example for us in the life of an ant. Everyday the ant goes to work. Everyday the ant is busy. And in the end, what happens?"
   "Somebody steps on him!" came a voice from the back of the room.

Visitor: And how many students are there in this school?
Teacher: About one in every five.

First boy: Where do all the bugs go in winter?
Second boy: Search me!
First boy: No, thanks. I just wanted to know.

A little boy came back from his first day in school and announced that he wasn't ever going back.

"Why not?" asked his mother.

"Because," he said. "I can't read, I can't write, and the teacher won't let me talk. So what's the use?"

Johnny: Hey, Tommy, aren't you coming out to play?

Tommy: No. I have to stay in and help my father with my homework.

What do you call the sweetheart of a ghoul?

A ghoul friend.

What comes out at night and goes "Flap! Flap! Chomp! Ouch!"?

A vampire with a sore tooth.

Little Tommy was telling his mother about his day in school. "Today our teacher asked me if I had any younger brothers or sisters, and I told her I was the only child."

"And then what did she say?" his mother asked.

"Thank goodness!"

Teacher: Can anyone tell me the meaning of "unaware"?
Pupil: "Unaware" is what you put on first and take off last.

What is a shark's favorite flavor of ice cream?
  Sharkolate.

Boy: How did you find the weather when you were on vacation?
Girl: Oh, I just went outside and there it was!

Jimmy: The police are looking for a man with one eye called Stanley.
Larry: What's the other eye called?

What do cannibals eat when they go on a diet?
  Pygmies.

Teacher: What can you tell me about the great scientists of the eighteenth century?
Pupil: They're all dead.

What's the principal part of a horse?
  The mane part.

Father kangaroo: Where's the baby?
Mother kangaroo: Oh no, I've had my pocket picked.

What did the Martian say to the gas pump?
   Take your finger out of your ear and listen to me!

What kind of hogs do you find on highways?
   Road hogs.

Knock, knock.
Who's there?
Nadya.
Nadya who?
Nadya head if you understand what I'm saying.

What comes after cheese?
   A mouse.

Why shouldn't you put grease on your hair the night before a test?
   If you do, everything might slip your mind.

What's a frog's favorite game?
  Croquet.

Rita: I got three cards on Valentine's day!
Freda: I got fifty.
Rita: Fifty! You lucky thing!
Freda: Not really. I could only think of forty
people to send them to!

Charlie: Everyone needs to feel wanted. My
dear old mom wants me.
Joe: The police want me!

Daphne: Do you like Morris Dancing?
Cynthia: No, he always steps on my toes!

Penny: I feel sorry for the Invisible Man.
Simon: Yes, he's just a shadow of his former self.

Jimmy: What's the difference between a mouse
and an elephant?
Johnny: I don't know. What is the difference?
Jimmy: Well, if you really can't tell, it's time you
wore glasses!

Howard: Do many people work in your office?
Philip: Only when they're not around the
watercooler.

Reg: Two from five equals one.
Teacher: Now you know that's not right!
Reg: Yes, it is.
Teacher: Give me an example.
Reg: The word "alone" has five letters. Take the first two away, and you're left with "one"!

Man visiting office: I'm in rather a hurry. Will Mr. Bell be long?
Secretary: No, he's rather short actually!

Why is night heavier than day?
  Because the day is light!

Gwen: Why do you carry an onion around with you all the time?
Bren: Because an onion a day keeps the doctor away—and everybody else, too!

Dry cleaner: Here's your coat, madam.
Customer: But there's nothing there!
Dry cleaner: Yes there is, madam. We used vanishing cream on a particularly stubborn stain that seemed to cover the coat, but it's all here!

Harry: Reg had his head in the clouds today.
Hugh: Oh dear, was he in a world of his own?
Harry: No, he was in a plane!

What did the frog say when it came out of the library?
  Read it, read it, read it!

Which animal needs oiling?
  A mouse, because it squeaks!

What do you call a comic that has legs?
  A stand-up comic!

Amy: I don't think Sue will make a good nurse.
Jane: Why not?
Amy: I had a cough the other day, and when I asked her for something to help it, she gave me a bandage!

Who would steal a cat?
  A cat burglar!

Unhappy farmer: I love my pigs, but I think they take me for grunted!

What kind of men are likely to fall at a girl's feet?
  Chiropodists!

What kind of combs do bees use?
  Honeycombs!

Alf: My son's a waiter.
Bert: Oh, he waits on tables, does he?
Alf: No, he waits for me to tell him what to do!

Customer: Waiter, there's a fly in my soup!
Waiter: We'll add it to your bill as an extra!

Len: My mother-in-law is coming to stay for the weekend.
Ken: Is she coming by train?
Len: No, by broomstick!

Where do you find a karate chop?
  In a Japanese restaurant!

What's the difference between a flea and a cat?
  Have you ever seen a flea with cats?

Why is the sun the same as rain?
  Because they both pour down on things!

Martha: It's been raining for two days nonstop!
Mildred: That's impossible, there's no way it can do that!
Martha: Why not?
Mildred: Because you can't have two days together. . . . There's always a night between them!

Julia: I went out in the rain yesterday and got soaking wet.
Lynn: Didn't you have your umbrella?
Julia: Yes, but when I put it up I couldn't see where I was going . . . so I fell in the river!

Patient: OK, Doctor, how do I stand?
Doctor: On two legs usually!

What was the first thing Elizabeth I did when she came to the throne?
   Sit on it!

Suitor: Mr. Brown, I'd like your permission to claim your daughter's hand in marriage.
Mr. Brown: Certainly, if you're sure, young man . . . but why don't you want the rest of her?

When did Adam appear on the Earth?
   Just before Eve!

What gets older, but doesn't age?
  A portrait!

What do people search carefully for, then get upset when they find them?
  Wrinkles!

What has four fingers and a thumb but is not a hand?
  A glove.

Father: Aren't you ashamed of yourself? You've been studying for three years and you can still only count up to ten. What are you going to do in life?
Son: I'll be a referee at boxing matches.

An apprentice witch doctor was learning the tricks of the trade from the old witch doctor.
  What did the old witch doctor tell him?
"Just watch what I do, then voodoo the same!"

Mother: Eat your spinach, it'll put color in your cheeks.
Daughter: Who wants green cheeks?

Hostess: Are you sure you can cut your meat?
Little boy: Oh yes, thanks. We often have it as tough as this at home.

What do you get when you mix eggs with soda?
  Yoke-a-cola.

Teacher: Correct this sentence. "It was me that spilt the ink."
Pupil: It wasn't me that spilt the ink.

Why did the rabbits go on strike?
  They thought they deserved a better celery.

Who always got his work done by Friday?
  Robinson Crusoe.

What is the difference between a ball and a prince?
  One gets thrown in the air, the other is heir to the throne.

Explorer: Is it true that an alligator won't bite if you carry a flashlight?
Guide: It depends how fast you carry the flashlight.

First racehorse: Don't you remember me?
Second racehorse: Your pace is familiar, but I don't remember your mane.

What makes a chess player happy?
  Taking a knight off.

Visitor: Tell me, why do you mix onions with the potatoes?
Farmer: Well, the onions will make the potatoes' eyes water, and I won't have to worry about a dry spell.

Why is it hard for a leopard to hide in the jungle?
  Because he's always spotted.

Teacher: Why are you running, Peter?
Peter: I'm trying to keep two boys from fighting.
Teacher: Goodness! Which two boys?
Peter: Larry and me!

First boy: Can you stand on your head?
Second boy: No, it's too high.

How can you tell if there's an elephant in your sandwich?
It's too heavy to lift.

How do you scold an elephant?
Tusk, tusk.

Customer: I'm afraid I can't pay for this suit for three months.
Tailor: That's all right, sir.
Customer: When will it be ready?
Tailor: In three months.

Knock, knock.
Who's there?
Hutch.
Hutch who?
Bless you!

Teacher: Name the highest form of animal life.
Pupil: The giraffe.

Two boys were walking past a sign in front of a school.
First boy: Do you know what P.T.A. means?
Second boy: I'm not sure, but I think it stands for Poor Tired Adults.

Knock, knock.
Who's there?
Mandy.
Mandy who?
Mandy lifeboats!

Boss: Do you feel this company's like one big family?
Employee: No—everyone's been pretty friendly so far.

Why was the sea angry?
  Because it had been crossed so many times.

What is the best exercise for losing weight?
  Pushing yourself away from the table.

Knock, knock.
Who's there?
Minneapolis.
Minneapolis who?
Minneapolis a day keep many doctors away.

Little boy: Was that policeman ever a baby?
Mother: Yes, of course.
Little boy: Oh, Mommy, I'd love to see a baby policeman.

What do you call a small judge?
   A little thing sent to try us.

When is it not lucky to see a black cat?
   When you're a mouse.

What do you get if you cross an elephant with a computer?
   A ten-thousand-pound know-it-all.

Teacher: Can you tell me where elephants are found?
Pupil: Elephants are so big they're hardly ever lost.

Which bird is not to be trusted?
   A stool pigeon.

When do elephants have eight feet?
   When there are two of them.

Teacher: Now, Sam, spell "mouse."
Sam: M-o-u-s.
Teacher: That's almost right. Now, what's at the end?
Sam: A tail.

How do you get a giraffe out of a cereal box?
  Read the instructions on the back.

Which were the two most important events in history that Charles I was responsible for?
  Charles II and James II!

Why did the cucumber look ill?
  Because it was green!

How did the prisoner see through the thick walls of his prison?
  He looked through the window!

Child: Daddy, there's a woman at the door asking if we'll give something towards the new church hall extension.
Father: Give her a brick.

Karen: What's the best way to start the day?
Carol: Do exercises?
Karen: No.
Carol: Have a good breakfast?
Karen: No.
Carol: What then?
Karen: Wake up!

What dogs lie in the road when it's been raining?
  Poodles!

Pattie: I nearly married Heart-throb Hank, the rock singer, you know.
Sarah: Gosh! Why didn't you?
Pattie: He didn't ask me.

Jenny: Did you hear about what happened to the jellyfish?
Julie: No, what?
Jenny: It set!

What game do you play with a racquet and a tomato?
  Squash!

Graham: My dad thinks old Mr. Black down the road is a vampire.
Gary: Why does he think that?
Graham: I heard him telling mom that Mr. Black's a pain in the neck!

Boyfriend: I'm giving you these sweets because you're the sweetest thing in the world.
Girlfriend: Thanks—I got you these nuts!

What is small and sharp and has one eye?
  A needle!

What's the difference between a chatterbox and a wooden box?
  You can shut a wooden box up!

Air hostess: What's the matter, sir? You look nervous.
Passenger: I am nervous. I don't like flying.
Air hostess: Well you should take a tip from our pilot.
Passenger: What does he do?
Air hostess: He shuts his eyes!

Doctor: I don't like the look of your fiancé.
Girl: So what—he's not marrying you!

Lucy: Does that chicken smell nice?
Flo: No, it smells fowl!

Why do people sleep well on April 1?
  Because they're tired out from marching for the past thirty-one days!

What can travel all round the country without moving an inch?
A railway line!

What did the suspicious window cleaner say to the window?
I can see right through you!

Stacey: My auntie thinks I'm a piece of fruit.
Tracey: What makes you think that?
Stacey: She keeps calling me the apple of her eye!

Ross: My cousin Ronnie married a woman.
Rick: I should hope so, he couldn't marry a man, could he?
Ross: My cousin Rachel did!

Why are boats and shops alike?
Because boats have sails and shops have sales!

What clothing does a house wear?
Address.

Knock, knock.
Who's there?
Havana.
Havana who?
Havana wonderful time, wish you were here.

Two monkeys were in a cage. One said, "I'm starving."

The other said. "Well, there's plenty of bread. Why don't you make some toast?"

The first monkey asked, "How can I make toast?"

The other replied, "Stick it on the gorilla."

Why is a fish like a person who talks too much?
Because it doesn't know when to keep its mouth shut.

What people travel the most?
Romans.

Knock, knock.
Who's there?
Tibet.
Tibet who?
Early Tibet, early to rise.

How can you spell jealousy with two letters?
   NV.

Why do you run faster when you have a cold?
   Because you have a racing pulse and a running nose.

When is a man not a man?
   When he turns into an alley.

Teacher: Did you see the eclipse of the moon last night?
Pupil: No, it was so dark I couldn't see a thing.

What would you get if you crossed a noisy frog with a shaggy dog?
   A croaker spaniel.

What is the difference between here and there?
   The letter T.

Jane: What do angels do when they are in heaven?
Mommy: They play harps and sing.
Jane: Haven't they any radios?

What happens when you phone a bee?
  You get a buzzy signal.

What piece of wood is like a king?
  A ruler.

What do camels have that no other animal has?
  Baby camels.

What pillar is never used to hold up a building?
  A caterpillar.

What would you get if you crossed a skunk and a banana?
  I don't know what you'd call it, but it would have a yellow stripe down the middle.

Teacher: What would you call a person who eats only vegetables?
Pupil: A vegetarian.
Teacher: And what about a man who eats people?
Pupil: A humanitarian.

How do rabbits travel?
   By hareplane.

Why are dentists moody?
   Because they always look down in the mouth.

When a girl slips on the ice, why can't her brother help her up?
   Because he can't be a brother and assist her, too.

First boy: My brother earns a living with his pen.
Second boy: Oh, is he an author?
First boy: No, he keeps pigs.

What do tailors do when they get tired?
   They just press on.

What would you get if you crossed a gorilla and a skunk?
   I don't know what you'd call it, but it wouldn't have any trouble getting a seat on the bus!

Bill: Hey, I heard something this morning that really opened my eyes.
Ben: What's that?
Bill: The alarm clock.

What's the easiest way to see flying saucers?
  Trip the waiter.

Where do all the good turkeys go when they die?
  To oven.

Why should you never upset a cannibal?
  Because you might end up in hot water.

What did the judge say after he'd finished work?
  It's been another trying day!

What is 10 + 5 minus 15? What is 3 + 6 minus 9? What is 17 + 3 minus 20?
  All that work for nothing!

Patient: Doctor, Doctor, I keep seeing spotted donkeys.
Doctor: Have you seen a psychiatrist?
Patient: No, I just keep seeing spotted donkeys.

Where do fish wash?
  In a river basin.

Who invented fractions?
  Henry the $1/8$.

Two pigeons watched in amazement as a rocket flashed across the sky.
1st pigeon: Wow! I wish I could fly as fast as that!
2nd pigeon: You would if *your* tail was on fire!

The manager of the International Periscope Manufacturing Company said today that his business is looking up.

Restaurant customer: Bring me a bottle of white wine—and I'd like it in an ice bucket.
Waiter: Wouldn't you rather have a glass, sir?

Benny: I'm looking for a silver wedding anniversary card for my wife.
Lenny: But you've only been married three years.
Benny: I know, but it *feels* like twenty-five.

How can you spot a shark owner in a pet shop?
  He's the one buying a two-mile leash.

Where would you find a vampire plant?
  In a bat-anical garden.

How does an elephant get down from a tree?
  He climbs onto a leaf and waits for autumn.

Knock, knock.
Who's there?
Eileen.
Eileen who?
Eileen on the fence and it breaks.

Customer: Waiter, this food isn't fit for a pig!
Waiter: Sorry, sir, I'll bring you some that is.

Why is an elephant gray, large, and wrinkled?
  Because if he were small, white, and round he
would be an aspirin.

Which glove is the correct one to wear?
  The right one!

What do you get if you milk a hen?
  An egg cream.

What's the longest day of the week?
  Wednesday, because it's got nine letters!

What is there a lot of in the Atlantic Ocean?
  Water!

Eileen: An apple comes under fruit, a cauliflower comes under vegetables, so what does an egg come under?
Helen: A hen.

Henry VIII (angrily): Send that woman to the Tower!
1st courtier: What did she do wrong?
2d courtier: She gave him a book on how to lose weight quickly!

When do teeth tell lies?
  When they are false!

What did the transverse rod say to the window?
  It's curtains for us!

Knock, knock!
Who's there?
Lettuce!
Lettuce who?
Lettuce pray!

What line has no beginning and no end?
A circle!

Man in hotel room: I think I'll take a shower.
Wife: But we've already got one at home!

What nuts can be found in space?
Astronuts!

What have a barmaid and a medium got in common?
They both deal with spirits!

Which snake is good at math?
An adder!

What did the disgruntled carpet say to the lady of the house?
I'm fed up with being stepped on!

What goes up and down, but doesn't move?
  A staircase.

Knock, knock.
Who's there?
Sherry.
Sherry who?
Sherry dance?

Doctor (to medical student): Now, Brown, it is clear from this X ray that one of the patient's legs is much shorter than the other. What would you do in a case like this?
Brown: I expect I'd limp, too, sir.

How can you tell the difference between a can of chicken soup and a can of tomato soup?
  Read the label.

Office manager: Look at all the dust on this desk. It looks like it hasn't been cleaned for a month.
Cleaning lady: Don't blame me, sir, I've only been here a week.

June: So I told my boss, either he takes back what he said, or I walk out.
Joan: What did he say?
June: "You're fired!"

What belongs to you, but is used more by others?
  Your name.

Why did the cross-eyed teacher lose his job?
  Because he couldn't control his pupils.

Knock, knock.
Who's there?
Water.
Water who?
Water be ashamed of yourself.

Knock, knock.
Who's there?
Thumping.
Thumping who?
Thumping green and slimy is climbing up your
neck.

*Why can only very small fairies sit under
toadstools?*
  Because there's not mushroom.

The Forestry Commission hired a man who could
chop down fifty trees per day.
  What was he known as?
  A good feller.

What happened when the girl met the goat in the dairy?
   He turned to butter.

Teacher: Your hands are very dirty. What would you say if I came in with dirty hands?
Pupil: I'd be too polite to mention it.

Cannibal to his daughter: Now that you're old enough, we must look round for an edible bachelor.

Why did the boy go to the country?
   He wanted to see the barn dance.

Knock, knock.
Who's there?
Enoch.
Enoch who?
Enoch and Enoch, but nobody opens the door.

What do you call a tug-of-war on December 24?
   Christmas 'eave.

What did they give the man who invented door knockers?
   The No-bell prize.

What shampoo do mountains use?
   Head and Boulders.

Knock, knock.
Who's there?
Juicy.
Juicy who?
Juicy what I saw?

Why do firemen wear red suspenders?
   To keep their trousers up.

What did the caterpillar do on New Year's Eve?
   He turned over a new leaf.

Knock, knock.
Who's there?
Isabella.
Isabella who?
Isabella not working?

Why shouldn't you believe a person in bed?
    Because he is lying.

A surgeon took his suit back to the tailor and complained: "It's all wrong!"
    "What's the matter with it?" the tailor asked.
    "I don't know," the surgeon replied, "it was all right until I took the stitches out."

Customer: Waiter, how do you serve shrimps here?
Waiter: We bend down.

Knock, knock.
Who's there?
Shirley.
Shirley who?
Shirley you must know me by now!

How do tailors feel when they're neither happy nor sad?
    Sew-sew.

What is the most important thing a witch learns at school?
    Spelling.

What color is a happy cat?
  Purrple.

A leopard visited his optician. "Every time I look at my wife I see spots before my eyes," he complained.
  "Well, what do you expect?" the optician scoffed. "You are a leopard."
  "Yes," said the leopard, "but my wife's a zebra!"

What happens when dawn breaks?
  It goes into mourning.

How can you tell if a vampire has been drinking your tomato juice?
  By the two tiny tooth marks on the can.

Why is a leaking tap like a horse race?
  It's off and running.

What do you get if you cross an owl with an oyster?
  An animal that dispenses pearls of wisdom.

What is black and white and blue all over?
  A zebra at the North Pole.

Why did the chicken sit on the axe?
  So she could hatch-et.

How can you tell an elephant from spaghetti?
  The elephant doesn't slip off the end of your fork.

Teacher: Tommy, spell the word neighbor.
Tommy: N-e-i-g-h-b-o-r.
Teacher: That's right, Tommy. Can you tell me what a neighbor is?
Tommy: It's someone who borrows things.

Mother: Now, dear, what are you going to do when you've had enough to eat at the party?
Paul: Come home!

How do robots cross a lake?
  In a row-bot.

What did the leftover turkey say when it was wrapped up and put in the refrigerator for the fourth time?
  Curses! Foiled again!

What do you get if you cross a chicken and a cow?
  Roost beef.

What is the best way to clean an aardvark?
  With aardvarkuum-cleaner.

Susie: What kind of fly can you spread on toast?
Shelley: I didn't think there was any fly you could spread on toast!
Susie: Oh, yes . . . a butterfly!

Patient: I've had this bad cough all week and it still isn't any better!
Doctor: Well, keep practicing!

Patient: Oh, I'm really nervous about my heart operation.
Surgeon: Don't worry, in all my experience as a heart surgeon, only one patient has died.
Patient: How many patients have you operated on?
Surgeon: You're my second.

Little boy: My daddy's a branch manager.
Old lady: Really? What kind of firm does he manage?
Little boy: None. He looks after trees!

Maggie: What are you doing with those banana skins?
Madge: I'm making something to wear.
Maggie: What can you possibly make to wear with banana skins?
Madge: Slippers!

If there are ten ducks swimming in a pond and a poacher comes along and shoots six of them, how many are left?
   None—the others swam away!

Alec: Paul the painter is in trouble for signing his name on his work.
Alan: But painters always sign their pieces of art.
Alec: Pieces of art, yes, but not the walls of somebody's house!

What do you call a little joke?
   Minnehaha!

Why do artists sign their pictures?
   If they didn't, you wouldn't be able to tell which way up they were supposed to be!

Tony: My dad can carry a tree in his hand.
Tom: I don't believe you ... what kind of tree?
Tony: A palm!

Brian: John Collins married ten people last week.
Derek: But that's against the law!
Brian: Not when you're a priest.

Jill: I'd like to see a nice, quiet game of tennis, but it's impossible.
Carol: Why is it impossible for tennis to be a quiet game?
Jill: Because the players always raise a racket!

Mother hen: Dinner's almost ready. Henrietta's laid the table.
Father hen: Why couldn't she lay an egg like everyone else?

What do fire-eaters suffer with most?
   Heartburn!

Robert: Do you believe in life after death?
Bill: No, what makes you ask that?
Robert: Well, why have you left everything to yourself in your Will?

A motorist was going the wrong way down a one-way street.
Policeman: Do you know where you're going?
Motorist: Yes, but I'm late. Everyone else is coming back.

Judge: Have you ever been up before me?
Prisoner: I don't know, your honor. What time do you get up?

Knock, knock.
Who's there?
Vera.
Vera who?
Vera interesting.

Where do sugar fairies live?
  Gnome Sweet Gnome.

Teacher: Steve, your essay on "Our House" is exactly the same as your sister's.
Steve: Yes, it's the same house.

Knock, knock.
Who's there?
Ozzie.
Ozzie who?
Ozzie you later.

Knock, knock.
Who's there?
Pecan.
Pecan who?
Pecan someone your own size!

Patient: Doctor, I've swallowed the film from my camera.
Doctor: Well, we'll just have to hope that nothing serious develops.

What do you call a man who leaves everything to his friends?
   Will.

What's the difference between a thief and a church bell?
   One steals from the people, the other peals from the steeple.

Teacher: How many fingers do you have?
Billy: Ten.
Teacher: Well, if one was missing, what would you have then?
Billy: No more piano lessons.

Mother: Sally is taking French, Italian, and algebra. Say good morning to Mrs. Jones in algebra, darling.

How do you run over an elephant?
Climb up its tail, dash to its head, and slide down its trunk.

"Mommy, I just took a splinter out of my hand with a pin."
"A pin! Don't you know that can be dangerous?"
"It's all right. It was a safety pin."

What are the noisiest things in space?
Shooting stars.

What do you call a nine-foot-tall canary?
Sir.

103

Mother: Did your boyfriend enjoy the meal you made him last week?
Daughter: I guess so, he said he hasn't been able to eat anything else since.

Andrea: You have the face of a saint.
John: Which saint?
Andrea: A Saint Bernard.

Mary: How can one person make so many mistakes in one day?
Alan: I get up early.

Teacher: If you had fifty cents and you asked your brother for another fifty cents how much would you have?
Peter: Nothing.
Teacher: That would mean your brother would have taken your fifty cents instead of giving it to you.
Peter: I didn't know you'd met my brother.

What does an artist like to draw best?
  His salary.

Filling in tax forms has always been a time-consuming job, so the income tax authorities have decided to simplify the paperwork. The form now consists of just two parts. 1) How much do you earn? 2) Send it.

Bill: Do you like working in the mortuary?
Ben: Well, it's rather a dead-end job.

Instructor: I've taught you all I know about parachuting. Now you have to make your first jump.
Recruit: But sir, what if the parachute doesn't open?
Instructor: If that happens, you'll find yourself jumping to a conclusion.

Mother: I think I'll take little Johnnie to the zoo today.
Father: I wouldn't bother. If they want the little horror they'll come and get him.

Dentist: Why exactly do you want sawtooth edges on your dentures?
Patient: I eat a lot of canned fruit.

1st football fan: I fell down and broke my leg before I came here today.
2d football fan: Are you in much pain?
1st football fan: I don't know. I'm not going to think about it till after the game.

Teacher: What is one quarter of one-tenth?
Pupil: Well, I don't know exactly. But it can't be worth bothering about.

Mother: Did you share those three lollipops with your brother?
Daughter: Yes, but it was difficult to divide three evenly, so I ate one first.

Mother: Why are you making faces at that bulldog?
Son: He started it.

Knock, knock.
Who's there?
Opportunity.
Don't be silly. Opportunity only knocks once.

Telephone operator: It's a long distance from London.
Man: Of course it is. Anyone knows that.

Neighbor: I'd like to give you a piece of my mind.
Naughty child: Think you can spare it?

Teacher: How many feet in a yard?
Boy: It depends on how many people are in the yard.

Rob: Did you mark the spot where the fishing was so good?
Bob: Yes, I put an X on the side of the boat.
Rob: Oh, that's ridiculous! I just don't believe you could be so stupid! What if we take out another boat next time?

Jane: What's the matter with Sue?
June: Oh, she's recovering from an unusual accident.
Jane: What happened?
June: A thought struck her.

Teacher: William, where was the Magna Carta signed?
William: At the bottom of the page, of course.

Man in restaurant: Waiter, will the band do requests?
Waiter: Certainly, sir.
Man in restaurant: Good—ask them to play cards, would you?

Val: Why were you so late for school this morning?

Hal: I squeezed too much toothpaste onto my brush, and it took me *ages* to get it back into the tube.

Boy: Dad, Dad, there's a man at the door with a funny face.

Dad: Tell him you've already got one.

Pupil: Which is correct—three and four *is* eight, or three and four *are* eight?

Teacher: Neither, you stupid boy—three and four make *seven*.

Woman: I'd like a new suit for my husband, please.

Tailor: I'm sorry, madam, we don't do exchanges.

Salesman: This machine will cut your work in half, sir.

Customer: I'll take two of them.

Boss (dictating letter): Sir, my typist, being a lady, cannot take down what I think of you, and I, being a gentleman, cannot say it out loud. But you, being neither, will be able to guess my thoughts.

General: What's your name, boy?

New recruit: John Smith.

General: Say "Sir" when you speak to a general, boy.

New recruit: All right, Sir John Smith.

Which is the best educated of all insects?
  A spelling bee.

Mother: Don't put that money in your mouth, there are germs on it.

Kid: Don't be silly, even germs couldn't live on this amount of money.

Mother: Antony, wash your face. I can see what you had for breakfast.

Antony: What did I have?

Mother: Eggs.

Antony: Wrong! That was yesterday.

Karen: Do you know her to speak to?

Julie: No, only to talk about.

What is the longest insect?
  The centipede, its body covers a hundred feet.

What is a witch called who lives in a desert?
  A sandwitch.

What do you do if you have a pack of cigarettes but no matches?

Throw one away, and you will be a cigarette lighter.

Karen, I'm burning with love for you!

Oh, Mark, don't make a fuel of yourself.

New father: Tell me, nurse, is it a boy?

Nurse: Well, *two* of them are . . .

How do you get down from an elephant?

You don't—you get down from a goose.

Judge: You are accused of driving up a one-way street.

Motorist: Well, I was only going one way.

Judge: Didn't you see the arrows?

Motorist: Arrows? I didn't even see any Indians.

The bank teller wasn't taking any chances when a lady customer asked him to cash a check. "I'm sorry, madam," he replied, "but we have very strict rules here, and I do not think you are one of our regular customers. Could you possibly identify yourself?

"That's no problem at all," replied the lady cheerfully, as she took a mirror out of her handbag. She looked long and hard into the mirror, studying herself from every angle and then replied: "Yes, it's quite all right, young man. It definitely is me!"

Teacher: Jim, can you name the four seasons?
Jim: Salt, pepper, mustard, and ketchup!

Simon: You must have paid the earth for that.
Susan: Oh, do you think it looks expensive?
Simon: No, dirt cheap.

What language do twins speak when in Holland?
  Double Dutch.

What will stay hot even at the South Pole?
  Mustard.

Where can you find five dozen keys that don't open a single door?
  On a piano.

What bird lives down a coal pit?
  A mynah bird.

Doctor: Take three teaspoonsful of this after each meal.
Patient: But I've only got one teaspoon.

What does a diver get paid if he works extra hours?
  Undertime.

I stayed in a small village last summer. My landlady kept animals. On the first day one of her chickens died, so we had chicken for dinner.

On the second day one of her piglets died so we had pork chops.

On the third day one of her ducks died so we had roast duck.

On the fourth day her husband died, so I left before dinner.

What's the biggest type of mouse in the world?
  The hippopotamouse.

1st critic: Did you see "The Hero's Lament" last night?
2d critic: Yes, I did.
1st critic: Who played the hero?
2d critic: Every man in the audience who stuck it out to the end.

Father: Your history teacher tells me you are her worst pupil.
Son: But it's not fair, Dad. She keeps asking me questions about things that happened before I was born.

Did you hear about the man who built a wooden moped with wooden wheels and a wooden engine?
  Wooden go!

Mr. Roberts: I'll pay you twenty cents to clean my car this week, and next week I'll raise it to thirty cents, Jon.
Jon: Right, Mr. Roberts—I'll start next week, then!

Teacher: How do you spell holiday?
Pupil: h o l y d a y
Teacher: The dictionary spells it h o l i d a y.
Pupil: Well, you asked how I spell it, not the dictionary!

Who was the best performer in the Bible?
  Samson—he brought the house down.

What's huge, purple and lives in the sea?
  Moby Grape.

What did the jack say to the car?
  Can I give you a lift?

Jim: Has your wife learned to drive your car yet?
John: Only in an advisory capacity.

George: What happened?
James: Flat tire.
George: You should have watched out for it. The guidebook said there was a fork in the road just about here.

Taxi driver: That'll be three-fifty, please.
Fare: Oh dear, I'm a bit short of money. Could you back up to two seventy-five?

Customer: Have you any caviar?
Waiter: No, but, I could let you have a bowl of tapioca and a pair of dark glasses.

Customer: A hamburger, please.
Waiter: With pleasure, sir.
Customer: No, I'd rather have onion and ketchup.

How do you make money fast?
  Glue it to your wallet.

*Did you hear about the cat that drank fifty
saucers of milk?*
  It created a new lap record.

How do hens dance?
  Chick to chick.

Teacher: Give me an example of a collective
noun.
Student: Er ... vacuum cleaner.

Visitor: A lot of important men have been born
in the town where I come from. Have many been
born in your town?
Host: Well, no ... but a lot of babies have been
born here!

Sally: Which people don't like bookkeepers?
Ann: I don't know.
Sally: Librarians!

Teacher: Johnny, when am I going to see an
improvement in your work?
Johnny: When you put your glasses on.

Joanne: Which part of going to school do you like best?
Penny: The holidays.

What do you call a disastrous cat?
  A catastrophe!

Diner: Waiter, what's this in my bowl?
Waiter: That's bean soup, sir.
Diner: I don't care what it's been. What is it now?

What do you call a camel with three humps?
  Humphrey.

Receptionist: Dr. Binga-Bonga will see you now.
Patient: Which doctor?
Receptionist: Oh no, he's fully qualified.

Did you know that dolphins are among the most intelligent of animals? Yes, within a week of their captivity they can train a full-grown man to stand at the side of their pool and throw them their favorite fish.

What is a fifth part of a foot?
  A toe.

Visitor: How many sheep do you have here?
Shepherd: I can't say exactly. Every time I start to count them all I fall asleep.

On which side does a chicken have the most feathers?
 On the *out*side, of course.

Teacher: Jane, can you tell me what a prickly pear is?
Jane: Two porcupines?

Policeman: I'm looking for a man with one leg called Forbes.
Informer: What's his other leg called?

Pupil: How can I improve my guitar playing?
Teacher: Try playing with the case on.

Manager: Have you considered early retirement?
Employee: Oh yes, I'm always in bed by ten!

Patient: Two coronation teeth, please.
Dentist: Coronation teeth? What do you mean?
Patient: Sorry—I mean crowns!

Polly: I've got a new job restoring antiques.
Molly: That's interesting—where do you work?
Polly: At the beauty clinic.

What goes putt-putt-putt?
  A bad golfer.

Doctor, Doctor, I feel like a deck of cards.
  Wait here—I'll deal with you later.

Lady: I would like a pair of crocodile shoes.
Assistant: What size is your crocodile?

Patient: My neck's as stiff as a pipe, my head
feels like lead, and my nose is all blocked up.
Doctor: I can recommend a very good plumber.

Teacher: Name five things that contain milk.
Girl: Butter, cheese, cream, and two cows.

Mother: Well son, how did things go on your
first day at school?
Son: Not very well. They say I have to go back
tomorrow.

Hospital visitor: Your wife Margaret must miss you a lot.
Hospital patient: No, she's a very good shot, that's why I'm here.

What made the inventor of the matchstick so pleased?
It was a striking success.

A tourist went into a seaside restaurant that boasted they could supply any dish the customer required.

"Right," said the tourist, "in that case I'll have a whale sandwich with ketchup, please."

A few minutes later the waiter returned to the table empty-handed.

"I'm sorry, sir," he said, "we've run out of ketchup."

Teacher: Smith, can you name five members of the ape family?
Smith: Easy—Mommy ape, Daddy ape, and three baby apes.

Keep smiling—it makes the grown-ups wonder what on earth you're up to.

David had been warned to be on his best behavior when his rich aunt came to Sunday lunch. All went well until they had finished their meal, when David turned to his aunt. "Are you going to do your party trick now?" he asked.

"What party trick is that, dear?" his aunt replied.

"The one dad told me about. He said you drink like a fish."

Where do vampires live?
  The Vampire State Building, of course!

What keeps jazz musicians on earth?
  Groovity.

Child: Dad, how do fishermen make their nets?
Father: Easy—they just make lots of holes and join them together.

The Hollywood film mogul was telling his assistant which leading man he wanted for his new movie, but the assistant was doubtful. "Don't you think he's a bit too caustic?" he enquired. To which the film mogul replied: "I don't care how much he costs. Get him!"

He: I believe in saying it with flowers.
She: But you've only given me one flower.
He: You know I don't talk much.

What is the opposite of sorrow?
　Joy.
What is the opposite of misery?
　Happiness.
What is the opposite of woe?
　Giddy-up!

She: You really mean you want to marry me?
He: Yes, I do.
She: But you've only known me three days.
He: Oh, it seems much longer than that. I've been working for three years in the bank where your father has his account.

Teacher: Give me a sentence which uses the word "archaic."
Boy: We can't have archaic and eat it, too.

Bill: I know a man called Archibald Trash. He wants to change his name.
Jill: I'm not surprised. What's he changing it to?
Bill: Arthur Trash.

Father: Why were you kept in late at school today?
Son: I didn't know where the Azores were.
Father: Serves you right. In the future, just remember where you put things.

Why do white sheep eat more grass than black sheep.

   Because there are more of them.

Father: How many times have I told you not to exaggerate?
Son: Five billion, three hundred forty thousand . . .

What's round and very bad-tempered?

   A vicious circle.

Len: I dropped my watch in the Falls three years ago, and it's still running.
Ben: The same watch?
Len: No, the Falls.

Teacher: What are your favorite numbers, Susie?
Susie: 147, 283, 781, and 41.
Teacher: Good—now I want you to add your favorite numbers together.
Susie: Er . . . I think the numbers I *really* like are 2 and 2!

Mandy: Swimming is excellent exercise—it keeps you slim, and is very good for the figure.
Sandy: Then why are ducks short and fat?

Mick: Are you taking the school bus home today, Nick?
Nick: No, my mom would only make me bring it back again.

Peter: Hello, this is Peter.
Paul: Hello. What can I do for you?
Peter: My car's broken down, and I'd like you to lend me one hundred dollars for the garage bill.
Paul: There must be something wrong with the line. I can't hear you very well.
Peter: I want to borrow one hundred dollars.
Paul: I still can't hear you.
Operator: Hello, this is the operator. I can hear him quite clearly.
Paul: Then you lend him the one hundred dollars.

Mother: I don't want you using those bad words anymore.
Son: But mother, Shakespeare uses them.
Mother: Then I forbid you to play with him again.

Husband: Why do you always give tramps a hot meal? They only expect a crust of bread.
Wife: I know, but it's such a treat to see a man enjoying a meal without complaining about the cooking.

Tramp: The lady next door gave me a piece of homemade pie. Will you give me something, too?
Housewife: I think I'd better give you an indigestion tablet.

When Adam met Eve what three words did he speak that say the same thing spelled backwards?
Madam I'm Adam.

What trees do fortune tellers like best?
Palm trees.

Bob Smythe was so rich that even the bags under his eyes had his initials on them.

What happens when a frog's car breaks down?
It gets toad away.

Knock, knock.
Who's there?
Little boy.
Little boy who?
Little boy who can't reach the doorbell.

Father: Well, kids, did you help do the dishes?
1st kid: Yes, Dad, I washed them.
2d kid: And I dried them.
3d kid: And I swept up the broken bits.

What ring is square?
   A boxing ring.

Rob: I've just come from London where I did a tremendous business deal. How much do you think I sold?
Bob: Oh, about half.
Rob: Half what?
Bob: Half of what you say.

Is this a secondhand store?
   Yes.
Good, I want one for my watch.

Boss: If Mr. Smith comes by today, tell him I'm out.
Secretary: Yes, sir.
Boss: Don't let him see you working, or he won't believe you.

What is never seen but often changes?
  Your mind.

What have clouds and horseback riders got in common?
  They both hold the rains.

Do you write with your left hand or your right hand?
  Neither, I write with a ballpoint pen.

Teacher: Hands up, all those children who want to go to heaven.
(Everyone puts their hands up except Karen.)
Teacher: Karen, don't you want to go to heaven?
Karen: Yes, but my mother told me to go straight home.

Marriage is like a fortress.
  Those who are in wish to get out and those who are out wish to get in.

Every man has a price, every woman has a figure.

What did Tarzan say when he saw a big pink elephant wearing sunglasses coming down the road towards him?

Nothing—he didn't recognize him.

Bill: What do you call a couple of people with food poisoning?
Ben: I don't know.
Bill: Sam and Ella.

Bob: The new lion tamer has been mauled by one of the lions.
Rob: Was he clawed?
Rob: I don't know his name—we weren't introduced.

What flies and wobbles?

A jellicopter.

At the wedding the usher stopped a woman and enquired, "Are you a friend of the groom?"

"Of course not, I'm the bride's mother," came the reply.

I hear your first two husbands died of food poisoning. What caused it?

Poisonous mushrooms.

What did your third husband die of?

He wouldn't eat his mushrooms.

Guest: Are the sheets clean?

Hotel receptionist: Of course they are, we had them washed yesterday. If you don't believe me, feel them, they're still damp.

"Come on, Timothy, kiss Aunty Eileen."

"Why, Mom, I ain't done nothing wrong."

Mark: I've lost my cat.

John: Put an ad in the paper.

Mark: Don't be silly, it can't read.

Three rather deaf friends met in the middle of town.

"Windy, isn't it?" said one.

"No, it's Thursday," said the second.

"So am I," said the third. "Let's go for a drink."

What made the fly fly?

The spider spied'er.

What makes a traffic signal turn red?

Having to change in front of so many people.

How does a Scout start a fire in less than a minute with just two sticks?

By making sure one of them is a matchstick.

Son: Can I have five cents, dad?
Father: Don't you think you're getting a bit big to ask for five cents?
Son: Perhaps you're right. Can I have half a dollar?

What did the hippie say to the invisible man?

"Hey man, you're out of sight!"

Porter: Do you want me to call you a taxi?
Tourist: Yes.
Porter: You're a taxi.

Patient: Doctor, I keep thinking I'm a goat.
Doctor: Really? How long have you had this feeling?
Patient: Ever since I was a kid.

Man in bar: How dare you swear in front of my wife?
Drunk: Why, was it her turn?

What type of cake do small boys dislike?
   A cake of soap.

Woman: I'd like a dog licence for my dog, please.
Clerk: Certainly. Name please?
Woman: Rags.

Recipe:
   "To add extra spice to your apple pies, add a teaspoon of cinnamon, a few grates of fresh nutmeg and two or three gloves."

Proud car owner: You'd never think my car was secondhand, would you?
Unimpressed friend: No, it looks as if you made it yourself.

Who shaves the hairs off oranges?
   The barber of Seville!

What's the easiest way to keep a stiff upper lip?
   Starch your moustache!

What happens when two oxen bump into each other?
    An oxident.

What day of the year is a command to go forward?
    March 4th.

Mother: If you wanted to go to the park with those boys, why didn't you come and ask me first?
Paul: Because I wanted to go to the park with those boys.

Mother: Do you know where bad little boys go?
Stewart: Yes, they go everywhere.

How come most dentists are fat?
    Almost everything they touch is filling.

Aunt Emilia had had a parrot for twenty-five years, and all that time she had been trying to teach it to talk. The parrot never said a word, until one day, as she fed it a piece of fruit, it suddenly squawked:

"Ugh! I'm not eating that muck! It's got a maggot in it!"

Aunt Emilia was astonished. "I've had you twenty-five years," she said, "and you've never once said a word. Why start now?"

"Well," replied the parrot, "the food's always been all right before."

Shop teacher: What are you making, boy?
Boy: A portable, sir.
Shop teacher: A portable what?
Boy: I'm not quite sure, sir. So far I've just made the handles.

Grocer (to small boy loitering near his fruit stand): "Were you trying to take a pear?"
Small boy: "No, I was trying not to."

How many apples can you put into an empty box?

One. After that the box isn't empty.

What did the captain say to his men before setting sail around the world?

Get in!

What letters of the alphabet would frighten a burglar?
OICU!

John: The Chinese have a custom of settling all their debts on New Year's Day.
Simon: So I understand, but they don't have Christmas the week before, do they?

Jim: I can't come to your party tonight, I'm going to see *Romeo and Juliet*.
Tim: That's okay, bring them along, too. The more the merrier!

Nat: That girl is a peach.
Mat: You mean she's nice?
Nat: No, she's got a heart of stone.

Knock, knock.
Who's there?
Toby.
Toby who?
Toby or not Toby, that is the question.

Teacher: Susan, say something beginning with "I."
Susan: I is . . .
Teacher: No, I am, not I is.
Susan: OK, I am the ninth letter of the alphabet.

What's worse than being with a fool?
  Fooling with a bee.

Teacher: Where is your textbook, John?
John: I ain't got one.
Teacher: Not ain't got one—it's haven't got one.
I haven't got one, we haven't got one, they
haven't got one.
John: Who *has* got one, then?

When is a blue book not a blue book?
  When it is read.

Tim: Have you ever seen a catfish?
Tom: Yes.
Tim: How did it hold the rod?

What kind of car does an electrician drive?
  A Voltswagen.

Woman: Doctor, this new diet you've put me on
makes me very irritable. The other day I got so
angry with a saleswoman that I bit her ear off.
Doctor: Well, don't worry. It's only about one
hundred calories.

Ben: We've got a new dog. Why don't you come and play with him?

Ken: Well, I don't know. I've heard him snarling and growling, and he doesn't seem very friendly. Does he bite?

Ben: That's what I want to find out.

What goes tick-tock-woof?
  A watchdog.

Did you hear about the human cannonball?
  He got fired.

Teacher: When was Rome built?

Boy: At night.

Teacher: Who told you that?

Boy: You, sir, you said Rome wasn't built in a day.

One day two mothers and two daughters went shopping. Each of them purchased a dress. But only three dresses were purchased. Why is that?

  Because there were only three shoppers: a girl, her mother, and her grandmother.

Wrestler's son: My dad's stronger than yours.

Policeman's son: Oh yeah? My dad can hold back a line of cars with one hand.

Inscription on a hypochondriac's tombstone: "See, I told you I was ill."

What did the hijacker sing to the astronaut?
Fly me to the moon.

Which fish make shoes?
Sole and eel.

What makes a bachelor such a smart man?
He has never been miss taken.

What goes hoe, hoe, hoe?
A laughing gardener!

John: In Hawaii the weather is the same all year round.
Susan: How do people start their conversations, then?

Bill: Our son wanted to be a doctor, but he failed the entrance exam for the Medical School. Still, he's doing the next best thing now.
Will: What's that?
Bill: He's an undertaker!

Little girl: Auntie Pat's getting you a wooden spoon for your birthday, Daddy.
Father: Why does she think I need a wooden spoon?
Little girl: Well, she says you're always stirring things up!

Angela: I'm going to meet my dad at the airport.
Wendy: But I thought you already knew him!

Mark: The ocean makes me think of pirates, buried treasures and battles on the high seas. . . . What does it make you think of?
Mick: Being sick!

Manager: Your name should be up in lights.
Singer: Oh, do you really think so?
Manager: Yes, that way people will know which show not to see!

What do most boys find easy to get into but very hard to get out of?
   Trouble.

When does a boy get wet?
   When he falls into water.

Why do storks only lift one leg?
   Because if they lifted the other leg they would fall down.

Have you heard the joke about the quicksand?
   It takes a long time to sink in.

Does your husband ever get a hangover?
   No, he's always drunk.

Tim: Did you hear about Charlie Jones?
Jim: No.
Tim: He invested his life savings in a newspaper stand.
Jim: Well, what happened?
Tim: It blew away.

Fred: Do you think this frog can jump higher than a house?
Ed: No, silly! Houses can't jump at all!

Marty (staring at Arty's empty canvas): What are you doing?
Arty: I've just painted a picture of a cow chewing grass.
Marty: Where's the grass?
Arty: The cow ate it.
Marty: Where's the cow?
Arty: Oh, he's gone—there was no point in him hanging around when there was no grass to eat.

How many sides has a football?
   Two—inside and outside!

How did the Vikings keep in touch with one another?
   They used Norse Code!

Tramp: Would you give me a quarter for a pie, lady?
Woman: I don't know—I'd have to see the pie first.

What does everyone need, everyone gives, we sometimes ask for, but very seldom take?
   Advice.

To whom do people always take off their hats?
   Hairdressers.

Why do you always find things in the last place you look?
   Because when you have found it you stop looking.

What's the best way to talk to a giant?
    Use big words.

Ann: Why did you call your new dog Ginger?
Nan: Because he snaps!

Mommy: Whoever taught you to use that dreadful word?
Sonny: Santa Claus did, mommy.
Mommy: Santa Claus?
Sonny: Yes, he used it when he stubbed his toe on a chair in my bedroom on Christmas Eve.

Mother: Ann, where is your sister?
Ann: In the next room.
Mother: Well, go and see what she's doing and tell her to stop it!

Son: Mother, I just knocked down the ladder that was standing up against the side of the house.
Mother: Go and tell your father.
Son: He knows all about it. He's hanging onto the roof!

Father: How many letters are there in the alphabet?
Son: I'm not sure.
Father: You are ten years old and you don't know how many letters are in the alphabet?
Son: Well, you are forty-six, and you don't know.

Angela was saying her prayers quietly.
"I can't hear you," remarked her mother.
"I'm not talking to you," came the reply.

The joke you just told me isn't funny one bit.
It's pointless and dull, wholly lacking in wit.
It's so old and so stale, it's beginning to smell.
Besides, it's the one *I* was going to tell.

Woman: I can't stand people who cook from the dining room table any more than my husband can stand backseat drivers.

How did the suspenders break the law?
They held up someone's trousers.

A lady was buying her Thanksgiving turkey, but she didn't seem pleased with the one the butcher offered her. "It's not big enough," she said. The butcher knew that it was his last bird, but he pretended that he would go and have a look in the back room. What he actually did there was to ruffle the feathers of the first turkey, and put it in a bigger bag.

"Oh, that's fine," said the lady, when he showed it to her. "I'll take them both."

A night watchman went to his doctor because he wanted something to improve his eyesight in the dark. "Be like a rabbit," said the doctor, "and eat lots of carrots." Well, the night watchman did as he was told, and his eyesight did improve slightly. Trouble was, he kept tripping over his ears.

John: When I was on vacation abroad I went fishing in one of those glass-bottom boats.
Jim: What exactly is the point of those boats?
John: So the fish can see how big the man is that they got away from.

Wireless operator: There's a tramp steamer signalling us.
Captain: What do they want?
Wireless operator: They want ten cents for a cup of coffee.

Silvia: Daddy, why have you got so many gray hairs?

Father: Probably because you are so naughty.

Silvia: You must have been terribly naughty when *you* were a little boy.

Father: Whatever makes you think that?

Silvia: Look what you did to Grandmother's hair!

Comedian: Laughter is a wonderful thing, or so other comedians tell me.

Girl: I suffer from dandruff.

Hairdresser: Oh, tell him to go away, then.

How can you stop yourself from dying?
   Stay in the living room.

What did the cobbler say to the birds watching him eat?
   Shoo.

Dan: You remind me of the sea.

Ann: Because I'm wild, romantic, and exciting?

Dan: No, you make me sick.

What kind of cat do you always find in a library?
   A catalogue.

What is the best day for making eggs and bacon?
  Fri-day.

Man on line: How long will the next bus be?
Man behind him: Oh, about twenty feet, I
should think.

Diner: I'd like to order a piece of steak as tough
as old boot leather, some peas as hard as bullets,
and a helping of greasy french fries.
Waiter: I'm sorry, sir, we couldn't possibly serve
you anything like that.
Diner: Why not? That's what you gave me
yesterday.

Ann: I'm glad I wasn't born in France.
Dan: Why's that?
Ann: I can't speak French.

Rick: I've just got a job at the Eagle Laundry.
Dick: That sounds dangerous.

The applicant for the chauffeur's job was
undergoing a difficult interview. He answered all
the questions about driving correctly, and the
interviewer told him that he had almost had the
job. "There's just one more test," she said. "And
it's a toughie. Let's see you fold this road map."

A guide was showing an old lady around a zoo, and they came to an enclosure of kangaroos. "These, madam, are natives of Australia," said the guide. "Goodness me," replied the lady, "and to think my sister married one of those."

Boy: My sister married an Irishman.
Lady: Oh, really?
Boy: No, O'Grady.

Mr. Stone: How is Mrs. Wood and all the little splinters?
Mr. Wood: Fine, thank you. And how is Mrs. Stone and all the little pebbles?

Mr. Murphy: If you had five cents in one pocket and eighteen cents in the other pocket how much money would you have?
Boy: None. I'd have somebody else's trousers on.

Fire chief to recruit: Suppose all the fire engines are out at a fire and another fire is reported. What would you do?
Recruit: I'd make sure I kept it going till you got there.

Antony: Going to have dinner anywhere tonight?
Susan: Why no, not that I know of.
Antony: Gee, you'll be hungry by tomorrow morning.

A mother said to her two daughters, who had a habit of borrowing things without asking, "I'm hiding this umbrella in here so you can't find it."

What sits in a bowl and shouts for help?
A damson in distress.

Man in water: "Help! I can't swim."
Passerby: "So what? I can't play the piano, but I don't go shouting about it."

Molly: What's the best thing you've seen on TV this week?
Dolly: The "off" switch.

A man found a kangaroo in a park. "What shall I do with him?" the man asked a policeman.

"Take him to the zoo," the policeman replied.

The next day the policeman walked through the park again, and saw the man, who still had the kangaroo with him. "Didn't I tell you to take that kangaroo to the zoo?" the policeman asked.

"That's right," the man replied. "But I took him to the zoo yesterday, so today we're going to the movies instead."

Car owner: Have you got my car started?
Mechanic: No, sir, your battery's flat.
Car owner: What shape *should* it be?

What do you do to a kangaroo with appendicitis?
   You hoperate on him.

A man tried to sell his neighbor a dog, promising that the dog could talk, but the man refused to believe him. Suddenly the dog spoke. "Please buy me," the dog pleaded. "My master is cruel and never feeds me, even though I'm the richest dog in the world."

"So he *can* talk!" said the neighbor. "Now why would you want to sell such a great dog?"

"Because he tells such awful lies," the man replied.

What kind of driver never gets a parking ticket?
  A screwdriver.

Mrs. Tall had a very clever pet parrot, and when her friend Mrs. Small came to tea she could not resist showing him off.

"If you pull this little string on his right leg," explained Mrs. Tall, "he'll sing the national anthem. And if you pull the string on his left leg he'll sing 'Roll Out The Barrel.'"

"That's amazing," replied Mrs. Small. "What happens if you pull both strings at once?"

"I fall off my perch, you silly old bat," replied the parrot.

Who wrote "Great Eggspectations"?
  Charles Chickens.

Fred: I've just been fishing. I caught a trout, a salmon, and a potfer.
Ed: What's a potfer?
Fred: Cooking the fish in!

Doctor to Roman legionary: Deep breath, then count to XCIX!

A British tourist in America went on a day trip to Boot Hill and was surprised that so many of the outlaws had been hanged. "Did they hang people very often?" the tourist asked an old prospector.

"Nope," drawled the old-timer, "just the once."

Customer: I'd like two lean pork chops, please.
Butcher: Certainly, madam, which way do you wish them to lean?

What did the father ghost tell his son?
  Spook only when you are spoken to.

What did the alarm clock say when it fell into the water?
  I'm wringing wet.

Policeman: After the way you have just driven, I will have to introduce you to Miss Eliza.
Drunken driver: That's very kind of you. What's her first name, to make it less formal?
Policeman: Breath-Eliza.

What do you call two cows that live together?
  Pen pals.

Why won't the two elephants go into the swimming pool together?
  They only have one pair of trunks between them.

Which Indian tribes have the most lawyers?
  The Sioux.

What makes Wales gradually sink into the sea?
  All the leeks.

Mother: Auntie will never kiss your dirty face.
Boy: That's what I figured.

A mother was taking her two little boys, Jon and Don, on a journey by train. Jon had been annoying her all day, asking question after question. Eventually he said: "Mommy, what was the name of the last station?" And she replied: "I don't know. Don't bother me now. Can't you see I'm reading?" Jon settled back into his seat, and said: "It's a pity you don't know. 'Cause that's where Don got off."

Why is it hard to talk when there's a goat around?
   Because he's always butting in.

1st boy: My dad threatens me with his belt when I'm naughty.
2d boy: Does he ever use it?
1st boy: No, when he takes his belt off his trousers fall down.

Did you hear about the angry flea?
   It was hopping mad.

Employee: Can I have tomorrow off to take my mother-in-law shopping?
Boss: No, you can't, we're much too busy.
Employee: Thank you, sir, I knew you wouldn't let me down.

Foreman: Why do you only carry half as much as the others?
Worker: I guess the others are too lazy to make two trips.

A legend is a lie that has attained the dignity of age.

Where do fish raise money?
  In a prawn shop.

Where do cows go for their holidays?
  Moo York.

First snake: Is our bite poisonous?
Second snake: Why?
First snake: I've just bitten my lip.

What would you get if you crossed a sheep with a kangaroo?
  A wool jumper.

Policeman at door (shouting): Madam, your husband has just been run over by a steamroller.
Voice from inside the house: Slip him under the door, will you—I'm in the bath.

What kind of doctor treats ducks?
  A quack.

Hickory, dickory, dock,
The mice ran up the clock,
The clock struck one
—so the others all ran away.

Mother: Jane, you know you're not supposed to eat peas with your knife.
Jane: I know, Mother, but my fork leaks.

Mother: Timothy's only a year old now, but he's been walking since he was six months old.
Other mother: Oh, really? Isn't he tired?

Tom: Jane won't marry me after all.
Jerry: But didn't you tell her about your rich uncle and all the money he'd give you?
Tom: Yes, of course I did. She's going to marry *him.*

Customer: Is there any soup on the menu today?
Waiter: There was, but I wiped it off.

Customer: Waiter, I don't like the look of this cod.
Waiter: If it's looks you're after, why not eat the goldfish?

Adam: We learned all about Columbus today. He traveled thousands of miles on a galleon.
Eve: Don't believe everything people tell you about these foreign cars.

Notice in a restaurant:
IT IS BETTER TO FIND A HAIR IN YOUR SOUP THAN SOUP IN YOUR HAIR.

Boss: Everything in this factory is electrical.
Worker: Well the low salary gave me a shock, that's for sure.

Teacher: We teachers all call your son our wonder child.
Mother: That's very nice to hear.
Teacher: Yes, we all wonder if he's ever going to learn anything.

Two hundred passengers settled back in their seats for the first scheduled flight of "Vacation Moon," a rocket ship taking tourists into space. The rocket lifted off, and after about ten minutes' flight a voice began to speak over the loudspeakers. "Ladies and gentlemen, welcome to this historic flight. We are at present cruising at three thousand miles, and I would like to take this opportunity to tell you a little about the ship. First of all, we have eliminated all possibility of human error, and the ship is crewed entirely by robots. Therefore there is nothing at all that can possibly go wrong . . . go wrong . . . go wrong . . ."

Mrs. Jones turned to her son, James. "Here is some candy," she said. "I want you to share it with your sister, Susan. Will you do that?"

James nodded his head and off he went.

Later, when James and Susan came in for lunch, Mrs. Jones spoke to Susan. "I asked James to share the candy with you—did he?"

"Oh, yes," said Susan. "He ate the candy, and I got the wrappers."

What do you get if you cross elephants with goldfish?

Swimming trunks.

Molly: I went to the dentist yesterday.
Polly: Does your tooth still ache?
Molly: I don't know—the dentist kept it.

Customer: I'd buy that dog, but its legs are too short.
Pet shop owner: Too short? They all touch the floor, don't they? What more do you want?

How do you know when it's raining cats and dogs?
There are lots of poodles on the road.

Ten girls were sheltering under a large umbrella. Why didn't any of them get wet?
It wasn't raining.

What did the orangeade say to the water?
I'm diluted to meet you.

Tourist: Tell me, whose skeleton is that?
Guide: That is William Shakespeare's skeleton.
Tourist: Then whose is that smaller skeleton beside it?
Guide: That is the skeleton of William Shakespeare when he was a small boy.

Dick and Mick shared a field for their two horses. So that they could tell which horse was which, they tied a red ribbon around Dick's horse's neck.

But one day when they went to the field, the ribbon had fallen off. "How shall we tell the horses apart now?" said Dick.

Mick thought for a while. "I know!" he said. "You can have the black horse, and I'll have the white one!"

What do you give a sick bear?
   Lots of room.

What did the tonsils say to the gallstones?
   The doctor's taking me out tonight. Are you going anywhere?

Is it cold outside?
   Is *what* cold outside?

When is a boat affectionate?
   When it hugs the shore.

What makes the Tower of Pisa lean?
   Too much dieting.

Newlywed wife: I baked a sponge cake for you today, but I'm afraid it was a total failure.
Newlywed husband: Why was that?
Newlywed wife: The grocer sent me the wrong kind of sponges. . . .

Seen in a local paper's report on a wedding:
"And all the bridesmaids had red noses."

A man was standing in the middle of the road sprinkling powder all around him. "What are you doing?" asked a passerby.

"I'm sprinkling some elephant powder around," the man replied.

"But there aren't any elephants around here," said the passerby.

"I know," the man said, sprinkling more powder. "Good stuff, isn't it?"

Which bird can lift the heaviest weights?
  The crane.

Granny wanted to send her granddaughter a gift.

The girl lived at the other end of the country, so Granny had to mail the gift. She made a coat for the girl, but was worried about the high cost of postage. This is the note she enclosed with the coat: "Dear June, here is a new coat for you—I hope you like it. I have left off the brass buttons to make the parcel lighter. You will find them in the left-hand pocket of the coat. From your loving grandmother."

What can hold things together yet keep them apart?
Mortar, when it's between bricks!

Ann: I bumped into Fran today.
Nan: Oh, was she pleased to see you?
Ann: Not really—we were both in our cars at the time.

Ann: What's your dog's name?
Jan: I don't know. He won't tell me.

Diner: How long have you been working here?
Waitress: About six weeks, sir.
Diner: Then I don't suppose it could have been you who took my order.

William Shakespeare was trying to write a new play, but somehow he just didn't feel very inspired that day. He was puzzling over the beginning of another speech when he suddenly looked down at his pencil. "That's it!" he cried. "2B ..."

Ben: That's a fine kite you've got—what kind of paper did you use to make it?
Len: Flypaper, of course!

What do you call a sleeping bull?
  A bulldozer!

What do you call an area where ghosts live?
  A terrortory.

Knock, knock.
Who's there?
The invisible man.
Well, tell him I can't see him.

What kind of a book gives you splinters?
  A log book.

Psychiatrist: You'll be glad to know that our sessions together have convinced me that you definitely haven't got an inferiority complex.
Patient: That's wonderful, doctor. What makes you so sure?
Psychiatrist: I know now that you really are inferior.

Patient: I keep thinking I can see into the future.
Doctor: When did this start?
Patient: Next Monday!

What man claps at Christmas?
  Santaplause!

See how I can count my way outside. There is my right foot. That's one. There is my left foot. That's two. One and two make three. Three feet make a yard, and I want to go out and play in it.

What room has no floor, ceiling, windows, or doors?
  A mushroom!

What do you do if you get a blue banana?
  Try to cheer it up!

What has a neck but cannot swallow?
   A bottle!

How do you make a jellyroll?
   Push it.

Why don't robots panic?
   They have nerves of steel!

Do robots have brothers?
   No, only *transistors*!

What has a thousand needles but cannot sew?
   A porcupine.

What has a foot on each end and one in the middle?
   A yard stick.

How long will a twenty-four hour electric clock run without being wound up?
   An electric clock doesn't need winding up.

Teacher: Finish off this sentence. People in glass houses . . .
Sarah: Should not undress with the light on.

Child: Mommy, is it dinner time?
Mother: Not yet, dear.
Child: Then my tummy must be fast.

What's green, sneezes, and holds a torch?
  The Atchoo of Liberty.

What word is always pronounced wrong?
  Wrong.

What is full of holes yet can still hold water?
  A sponge.

What man shaves more than ten times a day?
  A barber.

How can you fit a gallon of milk into a half-pint jar?
  Condense it.

What did the discoverer of electricity get?
  A nasty shock.

Teacher: Tommy, are you going to sleep back there?
Tommy: I'm trying to, but you keep talking and interrupting me!

Teacher: Can I have your homework, Simon?
Simon: I haven't got it.
Teacher: What do you mean? Why haven't you got it?
Simon: I made a paper plane out of it, and someone hijacked it!

What do you call a cowboy who's all in a stew?
  Hopalong Casserole!

What do you get if you lose a race run in space?
  A constellation prize!

What can you make that nobody else can see?
  A noise!

Wanda: A coward is like a stick of butter.
Vanda: Why's that?
Wanda: They both run when the heat is on!

What's red, squashy, and says "pardon"?
  A strawberry with hiccups!

Teacher: Now Maisie, tell the truth. Did your father do this homework for you?
Maisie: No he didn't. He tried, but Mom had to finish it.

Mother: How is Johnny doing with his trombone lessons?
Teacher: He's making very good progress.
Mother: That's a relief. I thought I was just getting used to it.

Why does a giraffe have such a long neck?
  Because his head is so far from his body.

1st picknicker: Are spiders good to eat?
2d picknicker: I shouldn't think so. Why?
1st picknicker: There was one in your sandwich.

Two customers were looking at brands of potato chips. Said one customer, "Is it my imagination, or are the chips getting smaller these days?"
  Replied the other: "It's these new microchips everyone's using."

What has two arms, two wings, eight legs, two tails, three heads, and three bodies?
A man on a horse holding a pigeon.

Why is the letter "P" like a Roman emperor?
Because it is near "O" (Nero).

Boring television personality: You've seen me on TV, of course?
Neighbor (not impressed): On and off.
Boring television personality: And how did you like me?
Neighbor: Off.

1st mother: My daughter's only four, and she can already spell her name backwards.
2d mother: Really? What *is* her name?
1st mother: Ada.

What did the mouse do when the other mouse fell in the river?
Gave him mouse-to-mouse resuscitation.

Did you hear about the scientist who crossed a crocodile with a parrot?

It bit his leg off and said, "Who's a pretty boy now?"

What part of London is in France?

The letter "N."

Teacher: Which is the richest country in the world?
Pupil: Ireland.
Teacher: Why do you say that?
Pupil: Because her capital's been Dublin for years!

Irate gardener: I'll teach you to throw stones at my greenhouse!
Boy: I wish you would—I keep missing it!

Customer: Bring me a pot of coffee.
Waiter: I'm sorry, sir. We only have tea. The coffee is completely exhausted.
Customer: I'm not surprised. It's been very weak for several days.

Customer: These oysters are very small.
Waiter: Yes, sir.
Customer: And they don't appear to be very fresh.
Waiter: Then you're lucky they're so small, aren't you?

Bill: I'm out looking for someone to lend me five dollars.
Ben: Well, you've got a nice day for it.

1st astronaut: Why don't we go to the sun instead?
2d astronaut: Don't be silly. If we went to the sun, we'd burn up.
1st astronaut: Not if we went at night.

Customer: Do you charge for gravy?
Waiter: No, sir.
Customer: Do you charge for bread?
Waiter: No, sir.
Customer: I'll have a bowl of gravy and some bread.

Mother: What do you want to take your cod liver oil with today?
Child: A fork.

Which is the fastest, cold or heat?
  Heat; you can catch a cold.

A barrel of beer fell on me this morning.
  You don't appear to be injured.
It was light ale.

Why do birds fly south for the winter?
  It's too far to walk.

Why do hummingbirds hum?
  Because they can't remember the words.

A boy sat on the curb of a busy street,
pretending to fish with his line down a manhole.
  An old gentlemen walked by and stopped to
look at the sad-eyed boy. "How long have you
been fishing?" the old man asked kindly.
  "All day," said the boy.
  The old man handed a quarter to the boy.
"And how many have you caught, son?" he
asked.
  The boy pocketed the coin and smiled.
  "You're the seventh," he replied.

Knock, knock.
Who's there?
Cook.
Cook who?
Oh, is it one o'clock?

What do ghosts eat for supper?
  Ghoulash.

169

Seen on a playground wall:
HUMPTY DUMPTY WAS PUSHED!

Jackie: Did Julie inherit her beauty?
Susan: Yes, her father left her his cosmetics factory.

Peter: How long will the next bus be?
Inspector: The same length as the rest of them.

Father: Tim, what is three times four?
Tim: I don't know.
Father: Haven't you done a simple problem like that?
Tim: We only count apples.

Mother: John, how was the test?
John: Oh, fine.
Mother: Then why did the teacher send this note home with you?
John: Mother, I said the test was fine. I didn't say anything about the answers.

History teacher: Why are the middle ages known as the dark ages?
Jennifer: They had so many knights.

Bill: My wife converted me from an atheist to a believer.
Priest: How did she manage that?
Bill: I never believed in hell till I married her.

Trixie: Did you hear about the robbery at the laundry?
Dixie: No, what happened?
Trixie: Two clothes pins held up a shirt!

Bertie: My Dad beats me every morning.
Gertie: Oh, no, why does he do that?
Bertie: He gets up at 7 A.M. and I get up at 8 A.M.!

First Indian chief: I wonder why Running Deer doesn't send smoke signals anymore?
Second Indian chief: Because he's got central heating now.

What made the pillow slip?
  It saw the bed spread!

Driver: Isn't it great speeding along like this? Don't you feel glad to be alive?
Passenger: Glad? I'm amazed!

He: Can you see the movie screen?
She: Yes.
He: Is your seat comfortable?
She: Yes.
He: Are you in a draft?
She: No.
He: Will you change places with me?

Famous actor: But I've signed your book before.

Little boy: Yes sir, but when I get ten of yours I can swap them for one of Robert Redford's.

Pat: What's bright purple, has twenty-four legs, and ears that stick two inches out of its head?

Pam: I don't know.

Pat: I don't know either, but there's one crawling up your arm.

Diner: This goulash tastes awful.

Waiter: That's funny. It has a new pair of goulashes in it.

1st cannibal: I don't like your friend.

2d cannibal: Well, just eat your vegetables then.

Stable boy: You're putting that saddle on the horse with the back at the front.

New rider: How do you know—you don't know which way I'm heading!

Eskimo boy: What would you say if I told you I'd come a hundred miles through ice and snow with my dog team, just to tell you I love you?

Eskimo girl: I'd say that was a lot of mush!

Joan: My husband got a bad sprain at football last week.
Jean: I didn't know he played the game.
Joan: He doesn't. It was his larynx he sprained.

Son: How much am I worth, Mom?
Mom: You're worth a million dollars to me, Son.
Son: Well, could you lend me five of them?

Interviewer: Have you ever faced a math problem which completely stumped you?
Famous mathematician: Yes, I have. I can't work out how, according to television commercials, eighty-five per cent of all housewives use one brand of detergent, and ninety-two per cent use another.

Mother: I've told you time and again not to speak when adults are speaking. You must wait until they stop.
Child: I've tried that. But they never seem to stop.

One flea to another: Shall we walk, or shall we take a cat?

What is the grocer's favorite dance?
   The can-can.

John had it last, Jane had it once. Boys and girls never have it, but Frank Jones has it twice. What is it?
The letter N.

What kind of raincoat do actors wear on a rainy day?
A wet one.

What kind of children does a stupid florist have?
Blooming idiots.

What is an astronaut's favorite plant?
Missile toe.

"Is ink very expensive, Dad?"
"No, son, what makes you ask that?"
"Well, I spilled some on the carpet, and Mom is quite upset about it!"

Father: Now then, son, I want you to be quite frank with me.
Son: But Dad, how can I be Frank when I'm really Michael?

Bert: When you are at work, are you covered by insurance?
Bill: No, overalls!

Betty: My brother's in the removal business now.
Millie: Which removal firm is he with?
Betty: The local disco—he's a bouncer!

When is it socially acceptable to serve milk on a saucer?
When you are serving a cat.

Where do dead pigs go?
To the sty in the sky.

I had to give up tap dancing.
I kept falling in the sink.

Knock, knock.
Who's there?
Dishwasher.
Dishwasher who?
Dishwashn't the way I shpoke before I had false teeth.

Look, I've got a new pack of jumbo-sized cards.
Big deal!

What do you get if you cross a cocoa bean with an elk?
A chocolate moose.

What do you get if you cross a sheep with a rain storm?
A wet blanket.

Man: I need a vacation. The pressure is beginning to get to me.
Friend: Why, what's the matter?
Man: Yesterday, when I got back to my office from having lunch, I'd left a notice on the door saying "Back in half an hour," so I sat and waited for myself!

Corporal: You can't go in that room, Private Jones, that's the Colonel's quarters.
Private: Then why does the sign say "Private"?

Judge: I find the defendant innocent.
Burglar: Thank you, judge does that mean I can keep the jewelery?

Patient: I feel like a rough sea.
Doctor: Now, calm down!

Boy to chimney sweep: Do you like your job?
Chimney sweep: Yes, it soots me!

But Dad, I don't want to go to Australia.
  Shut up, son, and keep digging.

Priest: Haven't you read the Bible?
Man: No, I'm waiting for the movie.

What always goes to bed wearing a fur coat?
  A polar bear.

First man: Can your wife make a good stew?
Second man: Are you kidding? The only thing she can stew is tea.

Have you ever had your ears pierced?
  No, but I've just had them bored off.

Fred: So you're making me manager of the doughnut shop?
Sid: Yes, of the hole works.

For all parents: If your son is of no earthly good make him an airline pilot.

Life guard: Swimming isn't allowed here after eight o'clock.
Girl: I'm not swimming, I'm drowning.

Mrs. Johnstone, why has your daughter just put her tongue out at the young man?

Oh, that's the new doctor.

Peter: You dance very well.
Diane: I wish I could say the same for you.
Peter: You could, if you were as big a fibber as I am.

Employer: Why are you late again?
Typist: I overslept.
Employer: You mean you sleep at home as well?

Where does Friday come before Thursday?
In the dictionary.

Where do snowmen go for an evening out?
Snowballs.

What makes a road broad?
The letter B.

Why is a horse like a baseball game?
They both get stopped by the rain.

198

Every time I get on a ferry it makes me cross.

Who is married to that hippie?
  Mississippi.

What is the saddest tree?
  The fir tree, it pines a lot.

What always ends everything?
  The letter G.

Townie: And about how many sheep do you
have altogether?
Yokel: Nine hundred and eighty-two.
Townie: Amazing. Did you count them all?
Yokel: No, I just counted all the legs and divided
by four.

Boss: My assistant is a miracle worker. It's a
miracle if he works.

What is the beginning of eternity,
The end of time, space, and minute,
The beginning of every end,
And the end of every race?
The letter E.

When will a net hold water?
  When the water is frozen.

What's yellow and always points north?
  A magnetic banana.

Who has large antlers and wears white gloves?
  Mickey Moose!

Door-to-door salesman: Hello, little girl, is your mommy home?
Little girl on porch: Yes.
Salesman: She isn't answering the door.
Little girl: Well, this isn't my house!

Auntie: Do you like sundaes, Bobby?
Bobby: They're okay, but I prefer Saturdays!

Luna: Why does your dog keep going around in circles?
Oona: He's winding himself up—he's a watchdog!

Chick: I want to go to the zoo.
Chuck: I don't think they'll accept you. They only take animals!

1st mother: I'm going to take little Jimmy to the mall for a change.
2d mother: Oh—what are you going to change him for?

Two ladies were driving along in a car. "Do you use your mirror much?" asked the passenger.

"Oh, no," said the driver, "I always put my lipstick on before I set off!"

Woman: Whenever I'm down in the dumps I buy myself a new hat.
Neighbor: So that's where you get them from.

What does a hard-working gardener grow?
  Tired.

How did Little Bo Peep lose her sheep?
  She had a crook with her!

What is an archaeologist?
  Someone whose career is in ruins!

Newsflash: A man is in the hospital after swallowing a dozen daffodil bulbs. Doctors say he'll be out next spring.

What does the government nail you with?
  Income tacks!

What did Adam do when he wanted sugar?
  He raised Cain.

John: Will you do my homework for me?
Sarah: No, it wouldn't be right.
John: Well at least you can try.

Why did the farmer call his piglet ink?
  It kept running out of the pen.

What have an acrobat and a whisky glass got in common?
  They are both tumblers.

Sales clerk: It probably took a thousand worms to make that silk dress.
Customer: Isn't it wonderful what they can train animals to do?

Never try to drink and drive, you might stop suddenly and spill some of it.

Why did the sleepy farmer take a hammer to the barn loft?
   So he could hit the hay.

Mom: Are you sorry you fought with Jimmy?
Joe: You bet I am—I didn't know he was having a birthday party next week!

Knock, knock.
Who's there?
Scot.
Scot who?
Scot nothing to do with you!

Len: Which bird can you make jam out of?
Ken: I don't know.
Len: A gooseberry.

Two male centipedes watched a female centipede walk past. One male centipede turned to the other and said: "There goes a nice pair of legs, nice pair of legs, nice pair of legs . . ."

A teacher was telling her pupils about the importance of wrapping up warmly on winter days, and to illustrate her point she told them the true story of her neighbor's little boy. The lad had gone sledding without his coat and gloves, and now he was in the hospital, recovering from an attack of pneumonia. "So," finished the teacher, "what have you got to say about that?" A hand shot up at the back of the class. "Who's using his sled?"

Ted: Did you hear about the man who knocked down a house with one blow of his hammer?
Ed: No.
Ted: Yes, he was the auctioneer.

Woman in grocery: Five pounds of potatoes— and I'd like some with lots of eyes.
Shopkeeper: Why d'you want eyes in them?
Woman: So they'll see me through the week.

"Have I told you about my wife? Her cooking's so bad she even manages to burn salads!"

Teller: I can't accept this five dollar bill, sir—it's a very bad forgery.
Customer: What do you mean—bad? It's one of the best I've ever done!

Tom: I wonder why babies cry so much?
Jerry: You'd cry too if you had no teeth or hair.

Customer: I'd like to buy a new bed.
Salesman: With a spring mattress?
Customer: Oh, no, I'd like to use it all year round.

Why do cows wear bells?
   Because their horns don't work.

Knock, knock.
Who's there?
Ken.
Ken who?
Ken I come in?

A man and his wife were in bed one night, when suddenly the wife woke up. "Fred, Fred," she said, "I think I can hear burglars! Are you awake?"
   "No," said Fred.

What's the hardest part about riding a bike?
   The pavement!

What's worse than biting into an apple and finding a worm?
Finding *half* a worm.

On which of his voyages was Captain Cook killed?
The last one.

What's the difference between a forger and a comedian?
One tries to make funnies, the other to fake monies.

When will water stop running downhill?
When it reaches the bottom.

What animal would you like to be on a cold day?
Otter.

What do you get if you cross the Atlantic with the Titanic?
Halfway.

Why aren't you going to grow cucumbers any longer?
  Because they are long enough.

Waiter: Don't complain about the coffee, you may be old and weak yourself one day.

What always works with something in its eye?
  A needle.

How can you make a snail fast?
  Take his food away.

Harry: Is it true you're not going to Florida after all?
Larry: No, it's Bermuda we're not going to this year. It was Florida we didn't go to last year.

Why did the man have to repair the horn of his car?
  Because it didn't give a hoot.

Boy: What's for lunch, Mom?
Mom: Thousands of things!
Son: What are they?
Mom: Beans!

What goes ninety-nine-bump, ninety-nine-bump?
A centipede with a wooden leg, of course!

What do you call a man wearing earmuffs?
Anything you like—he can't hear you.

Husband: Do you have a good memory for faces?
Wife: Yes, but why?
Husband: I've just broken your mirror.

Patient: Doctor, Doctor, everyone ignores me!
Doctor: Next!

1st prisoner: This time last year I was making big money.
2d prisoner: Yeah—half an inch too big!

Corporal leading soldiers into battle: Fire at will, men!
Private: But which one's Will, Corporal?

Customer: These kiwis are completely covered in rough hairs!
Grocer: What did you expect—a body wave?

Ron: Do you think insects have brains?
Don: Course they do—see how they always know when we're going to have a picnic?

Mrs. Larger had a baby. Who was the largest?
  The baby, because he was a little larger.

What goes down the stairs without moving?
  The railings.

What have a preacher and a tennis player got in common?
  Their service!

Boris: Are you good at making toast?
Cyril: Oh, that's a burning question!

Wife: My husband is a credit to the community—
he owes everybody money!

Man to doctor: I think I'm sick, doctor . . . at
least I hope I am. I'd hate to feel like this when
I'm well!

Is that a popular song she was singing?
  It was, before she sang it.

Judge: The next person in this court who dares
to utter a sound will be thrown out.
Prisoner: Me! Me!

*Why didn't the inept baseball player meet
Cinderella?*
  Because he missed the ball!

Samantha: Why are you dancing the Twist and
holding that jam jar at the same time?
Sam: Because it says on the lid "Twist to open"!

Jimbo: It's easy to forget a tooth when you have
it taken out.
Jumbo: Why's that?
Jimbo: Because it goes right out of your head!

*Why was the mathematics book feeling
disgruntled?*
  Because it had so many problems!

What often runs but never walks?
  Water.

If your uncle's sister is not your aunt, who is she?
  Your mother.

Teacher on nature walk: And this, class, is a
dogwood tree. I can tell by its bark.

Customer: Do you sell dog meat?
Butcher: Only if it comes with its owner.

John: God bless Mommy and Daddy and make James Henton the king of Spain.
Mother: Why?
John: Because that's what I put on my exam paper.

What did the candle say to his friend?
  Are you going out tonight?

What did the calendar say to her friend?
  I have more dates than you.

Doctor: What seems to be the trouble?
Patient: When I get up in the morning I'm always dizzy for half an hour.
Doctor: Try getting up half an hour later.

Teacher: Now, Damien, you must not resort to fighting. You must learn to give and take.
Damien: We did. He took my chocolate, and I gave him a black eye.

Teacher: Michael, stop showing off. Do you think you are the teacher of this class?
Michael: No.
Teacher: Then stop acting the fool.

Why do you say my grandfather's teeth are like stars?
  They come out at night.

Why are there no dogs on the moon?
  Because there are no trees on the moon.

How do you get a baby astronaut to go to sleep?
  Rocket.

Man: What's your remedy for insomnia?
Friend: Several glasses of wine.
Man: Does that work?
Friend: No, but it makes me happier to be awake!

Tillie: My husband wants either a nice comfy chair for his birthday, or something electrical.
Millie: Which are you going to get him?
Tillie: I'm going to combine the two and get him an electric chair!

What's the difference between a small man and a large man running in a race?
  The small man runs in short bursts and the large man runs in burst shorts!

What does someone checking the football results have in common with a musician?
  They both read scores!

Boy: Mom, what happens when a car gets so old and rusty that it can't move?
Mom: Someone sells it to your father!

Pat: Do you know which bus crossed the oceans without getting wet?
Matt: Sure, it was Christopher Colum-bus!

Boss: Where's my pen, Miss Smith?
Secretary: It's behind your ear, sir.
Boss: Come, come, I'm a very busy man—which ear?

Harry: I haven't slept for days.
Larry: Why—insomnia?
Harry: No, I only sleep at night!

Teacher: Your typing is improving, Sally, there are only fifteen mistakes here.
Sally: That's great!
Teacher: And now I'll look at the second sentence. . . .

Definition of budget: a system of worrying both before and after you spend money, instead of just after.

One wise cannibal toasted his mother-in-law for the wedding dinner.

Doctor: Well, Mrs. Smith, I haven't seen you for quite a long time.
Mrs. Smith: I know, Doctor, I've been very ill.

First mother: My daughter's away at college. She's very clever, you know. Every time we get a letter from her we have to go to the dictionary.
Second mother: You're lucky—every time we hear from our daughter we have to go to the bank.

What do you give a sick canary?
  Tweetment.

What game always has its ups and downs?
  Snakes and ladders.

I hear your brother fell into an upholstery machine.
  Yes, but he's fully recovered now.

Conductor on train: Don't lean out of the window, son.
Boy: Why not?
Conductor: We don't want any of our bridges damaged.

Secretary: What silly fool has put these daisies on my desk?
Boss: I did.
Secretary: Oh, aren't they lovely?

Musician: I play entirely by ear.
Critic: You ought to remember that people listen the same way.

Boring Hostess: It's beginning to rain. You may as well stay for dinner.
Guest: Oh no, it's not raining as badly as all that.

What has eight feet and sings?
  A quartet.

What always weighs the same, no matter how big it gets?
  A hole.

What did the ground say to the rain?
  If you keep this up my name will be mud.

Why is a mousetrap like measles?
  Because it's catching.

What would you have if you owned a cow and two ducks?
  Cheese and quackers.

Mom: Shouldn't you give your goldfish some more water, dear?
Child: Why? It hasn't drunk the last bowlful yet.

Doctor, Doctor, I've just swallowed a sheep!
  How do you feel?
Very baa-a-a-a-ad!

What should you give to underfed pixies?
  Elf-raising flour.

What are assets?
  Little donkeys.

What do you call a nut that has a bad memory?
  A forget-me-nut.

A woman wanted to visit relatives in Australia, so she rang a travel agent. "How long will it take to fly to Australia?" she asked.
  "Just a minute," the travel agent said, and went to consult his timetables.
  "Thank you," said the woman, and hung up.

THEY'RE MORE THAN
FUNNY...

THEY'RE LAUGH-OUT-LOUD
HYSTERICAL!

What made Kojak throw away all his keys?
  He didn't have any locks.

What caused the flood?
  The river got too big for its bridges.

What is a Chinese spy called?
  Peking Tom.

What can you break using one word?
  Silence!

Teacher: If we breathe oxygen in the daytime, what do we breathe at night?
Sam: Nitrogen?

How many insects are needed to fill a building?
  Ten-ants!

Postman: Do you think this letter is for you? The name is smudged.
Woman: Oh, no—my name is Jones!

Fisherman 1: Is this a good river for fish?
Fisherman 2: Must be—I can't persuade any of them to leave it.

Art teacher: But I asked you to draw a horse and cart, John, and you've only drawn the horse. Why?
Student: I thought the horse would draw the cart itself!

John: Darling, you must marry me. There can never be anyone else for me but you.
Jane: I'm really not sure. Why don't you find someone else? Some beautiful woman . . .
John: I don't want a beautiful woman. I want you.

"I hope it won't rain today," said the mother kangaroo.
"I just hate it when the children play indoors."

Dentist: Stop making faces and waving your arms around. I haven't even touched your tooth yet.
Susan: I know. But you're standing on my foot.

Joey: I can't put this model together.
Johnny: Why not? It says on the box that a child of five can do it.
Joey: That explains it. I'm twelve.

When will a cat not enter a house?
When the door is closed.

Mother: Jimmy, I wish you would run over and see how old Mrs. Brown is this morning.
Jimmy (on his return): She said it was none of your business.
Mother: But what did you ask her?
Jimmy: Just what you told me to. How old she was today.

Jane: I've been asked to get married lots of times.
Janet: Who asked you?
Jane: My family.

A little girl was talking to her mother about growing up.

"When I grow up, will my husband be a man, like daddy?" she asked.

"Yes dear."

"If I don't get married will I end up like Aunty Julie?"

"Yes dear."

"Oh, mommy, I don't think I want to grow up."

What makes rabbits have shiny noses?
   Their powder puffs are at the wrong end.

Patient: Is there something wrong with my heart?
Doctor: I have given you a thorough examination, and I can quite safely say that your heart will last as long as you will.

What happens when the human body is submerged in water?
   The phone rings.

What is large, gray, and wrinkled?
   An elephant.

Why isn't an elephant small, white, and furry?
   Because then it would be a mouse.

What can run fast but still stay in the same place?
   A car engine.

Customer: Give me something to eat, and make it snappy!
Waiter: How about a crocodile sandwich?

Man: I hate paying taxes.
Lady: A good citizen should pay his taxes with a smile.
Man: I tried that, but they insisted on money!

Waiter: Would you like an egg on toast, sir?
Customer: Why, haven't you got any plates?

Man: My wife said I look like a million.
Friend: Yes, and I bet she meant every year of it!

What did the hotel manager say to the elephant who couldn't pay his bill?
   Pack your trunk and get out!

Why did the girl put her watch in her back trouser pocket before sitting down?
   She wanted to be on time for her date.

Drunk driver: Have I just run over that large black cat with the white collar?
Companion: No, you've run over a priest!

Little Willy was shouting his prayers: "Please God send me a new football for my birthday."

His mother, overhearing this, said, "Don't shout dear, God isn't deaf."

"No, but Grandad is, and he's in the next room," Willy replied.

What is the representative of the waiters' union called.

A chop steward.

Why is a cowardly soldier like butter?

Both run when exposed to fire.

What is always taken in a hospital, but never missed?

Your temperature.

A very rich man was swimming in the ocean when he got into difficulties. A man dived in after him and dragged him to the shore. "I'll give you artificial respiration," said the rescuer.

"No, give me the real thing," said the rich man. "I'll pay."

The podiatrist's theme song: "There's no business like toe business!"

"The average child has a lot of willpower," remarked the doctor.

"They also have a lot of won't power," replied the mother of six.

When is a sailor like a plank?
   When he's aboard.

Mark: Do you love me?
Karen: Yes, dear.
Mark: Would you die for me?
Karen: Mine is an undying love.

Antony: Do you love me for myself or my money?
Sue: It's mainly you I care for. I care for your money only up to a point—the decimal point after the first five figures.

Have you heard about the dogwood tree? It's had six puppies.

When is silence all wet?
   When it reigns.

Which side of an apple pie is the left side?
   The side that hasn't been eaten!

Two little boys were paddling in the sea at a beach resort. "Golly, your feet are dirty!" said the first boy, looking at the second boy's grimy feet.
   "I know," said the second boy, "but we didn't come here last year."

Ed: Boy, these new shoes hurt!
Ted: No wonder, you've got them on the wrong feet.
Ed: But they're the only feet I've got.

Advertisement in newspaper.
VERY CHEAP COATS
LAST THREE DAYS

Dolly: Did you have a good vacation?
Polly: So so.
Dolly: Why, where did you go?
Polly: We went to a place called Venice, but it was flooded!

A small boy who visited the zoo told his mother he had seen a tail wagging without a dog. The mother, after inquiring what he meant, found that her son had seen a snake.

171

Will you remember me in a week?
Yes.
Will you remember me in a month?
Yes.
Will you remember me in a year?
Of course.
Knock, knock.
Who's there?
See, you've forgotten me already!

Judge: I'll give you three months or one hundred dollars.
Criminal: I'll take the one hundred dollars please.

Child: Why does Grandad still have candles on his birthday cakes?
Mother: He likes to make light of his age.

Tommy: I don't think our new math teacher is much good.
Tommy: Why not?
Timmy: Well, yesterday he told us that four plus one is five.
Tommy: What's wrong with that?
Tommy: Today, he says it's three plus two.

1st critic: Does that new play have a happy ending?
2nd critic: Yes. Everyone was glad it was over.

What ballet is the most popular with monsters?
Swamp Lake.

What did the mother elephant say to the naughty baby elephant?
Tusk, tusk.

Who won the Miss Monster of the Year competition?
Nobody.

What is another name for a wise duck?
A wise quacker.

Just think, John married Angela.
I thought he was only flirting with her.
So did he.

Farmer's wife: It's our twenty-fifth wedding anniversary tomorrow. Shall we kill a chicken?
Farmer: Why punish the poor thing for something that happened all that time ago?

I keep thinking today is Tuesday.
Today is Tuesday.
I know, that's why I keep thinking it.

Peter: My family can trace its ancestry right back to William the Conqueror.

Paul: Oh yes, you'll be telling me next that your ancestors were in the Ark with Noah.

Peter: Certainly not. My family had a boat of their own.

Sherlock Holmes: Watson, I deduce that you have put on your winter underwear.

Dr. Watson: That's astonishing, Holmes. How did you know?

Sherlock Holmes: It's elementary, my dear fellow. You've forgotten to put on your trousers.

How many balls of string will it take to reach Jupiter?

One, if it's long enough!

A driver appeared before the magistrate, accused of speeding. He pleaded not guilty, saying that he'd only been doing twenty miles an hour. "But how can you be so sure that you were only doing twenty miles an hour?" the magistrate asked.

"I was on my way to the dentist," the driver explained.

What's the time when the clock strikes thirteen?

Time to get it mended.

Jimmy had completed his first day at school. All the other children had gone home, but he still stood in the playground.

"Aren't you going home now, Jimmy?" the teacher asked.

"No," said Jimmy, "Mom says I have to stay at school until I'm eighteen."

If two's company and three's a crowd, what are four and five?
  Nine!

Angry conductor to train passenger: So your dog's eaten your ticket, has he? I think you'd better buy him a second helping then, don't you?

What do animals read?
  Gnus papers.

What are pigs' favorite pets?
  Hamsters.

Why were the flies playing soccer in the saucer?
  They were practicing for the cup.

Instructor to student driver: "Now remember, stop at red, go at green—and slow down when I turn white."

Boy (doing homework): Mom, where are the Andes?
Mom (harassed): I don't know! If you put things where they belong you'd know where to find them!

Father: Well, Susie, how did you enjoy your first day at senior school?
Susie: Great! The teacher really likes me—she kept writing kisses in my notebooks.

At an elegant cocktail party one of the guests suddenly let out a great big burp, which reverberated all around the room. The host was horrified. "You there!" he cried. "How dare you burp in front of my wife?"

"Oh sorry," said the guest. "I didn't realize it was her turn."

What's a caterpillar?
   A rich worm in a fur coat.

Why would George Washington find it difficult to throw a dollar across a river if he was living nowadays?

Money doesn't go as far as it used to.

What goes farthest the slower it goes?

Money.

What has no beginning, no end, and nothing in the middle?

A doughnut.

Lady: How much is a cup of tea?
Waitress: Fifty cents.
Lady: How much is a refill?
Waitress: Nothing.
Lady: I'll take a refill, then.

Auntie: Well, Jane, were you very brave at the dentist's?
Jane: Yes, I was.
Auntie: Then here's the dollar I promised you. Now tell me what he did.
Jane: He pulled out two of John's teeth.

During a terrible snowstorm a St. Bernard dog was sent out with the usual keg of brandy, to find a lost hiker. Two hours later the dog came back with its little barrel empty. Attached to its collar was a note: "Enjoyed the brandy. Next time could you please send a double!"

What happens to a man who doesn't know toothpaste from putty?
All his windows fall out.

What do Eskimos sing at parties?
Freeze a jolly good fellow.

1st fisherman: Did you get many bites today?
2d fisherman: Yes, forty-four.
1st fisherman: That's amazing! What were they?
2d fisherman: Four fish and forty mosquitos.

Customer: Waiter, this tomato soup tastes like dishwater!
Waiter: Sorry, sir, I must have given you the wrong bowl—the tomato soup tastes like sour milk.

Jon: Were you invited to Jim's party?
Ron: Yes, but I can't go.
Jon: Why not?
Ron: The invitation says 6 to 8, and I'm 9.

Which country has the best appetite?
   Hungary.

Man: Will I be able to read when I get my glasses?
Optician: Of course you will, sir.
Man: Oh good, I didn't know how to before.

Why does everyone understand a heavy snow fall?
   Because you can see the drift.

'Twas in a restaurant they met;
Romeo and Juliet.
He had no money to pay the bill,
So Romeo'd what Juliet.

What's a cannibal's favorite shampoo?
   One with plenty of body in it.

Why are contortionists thrifty people?
   Because they can make ends meet.

An elephant is sitting on a stool.
What time is it?
Time to get a new stool.

Ann: We go away every third year.
Nan: What do you do the other two years?
Ann: The first one we talk about last year's vacation, and the next year we discuss plans for the following year.

Women's libber: Why do we sing "a-men" instead of "a-women"?
Priest: Because we sing hymns, not hers.

What is too much for one person, enough for two people, but nothing for the third person?
A secret.

Knock, knock.
Who's there?
Ken.
Ken who?
Ken you lend me a dollar until pay day?

Customer: I would like some bits for my dog, please.
Butcher: Certainly, Madam—which bits are missing?

Patient: Doctor, I've just swallowed a bone.
Doctor: Are you choking?
Patient: No, I'm serious.

Optician: You need glasses.
Patient: But I'm already wearing glasses.
Optician: Are you? Then *I* need glasses.

Teacher: Jane, what are doubloons?
Jane: Silly twins?

What's the best way to get on TV?
Sit on the set.

What kind of clothing do lawyers wear?
Lawsuits.

When do your teeth do what your tongue is intended for?
When they chatter.

I'm very annoyed with that scale. I stepped onto it and it said, "One at a time, please"!

Waiter: How did you find the beef?
Customer: Quite by accident. I moved the potato, and there it was.

Customer: Do you have a book called "How to Become a Millionaire"?
Shop clerk: Who's the author?
Customer: Robin Banks.

When rain falls, does it ever get up again?
Yes, in dew time.

Teacher: What is the definition of an adult?
Pupil: Someone who has stopped growing upwards and started growing sideways.

What gloves can't be worn?
Foxgloves.

How does a vet look in a lion's mouth?
Very carefully.

What does every duck become when it first takes to water?
Wet.

What is sold by the yard and worn by the foot?
A carpet.

Housewife: You should be ashamed to be seen begging at my door.

Tramp: Oh, I don't know. I've seen much worse houses than this one.

Policeman: You were speeding.

Motorist: Sorry officer, I didn't notice the speedometer. I was too engrossed in my book.

What would you call a mischievous egg?
A practical yolker.

If your dog lost his tail where would you get another one from?
A retail shop.

Policeman: I am going to have to ask you to accompany me to the station.

Drunk: Why, don't you like walking around on your own?

Teacher: When was the Magna Carta signed, Maisie?

Maisie: At a quarter past twelve.

Teacher: At a quarter past twelve?

Maisie: Yes. 1215!